Hesitation

Recent Titles in
Contributions in Psychology

Hesitation
IMPULSIVITY AND REFLECTION

Leonard W. Doob

CONTRIBUTIONS IN PSYCHOLOGY,
NUMBER 15

GREENWOOD PRESS
New York · Westport, Connecticut · London

Library of Congress Cataloging-in-Publication Data

Doob, Leonard William.
  Hesitation : impulsivity and reflection / Leonard W. Doob.
     p.   cm.—(Contributions in psychology, ISSN 0736-2714 ; no.
  15)
  Includes bibliographical references.
  ISBN 0-313-27446-0 (lib. bdg. : alk. paper)
  1. Hesitation. 2. Impulse. 3. Introspection.   I. Title.
  II. Series.
  BF637.H46D66 1990
  155.2'32—dc20   90-32107

British Library Cataloguing in Publication Data is available.

Library of Congress Catalog Card Number: 90-32107
ISBN: 0-313-27446-0
ISSN: 0736-2714

First published in 1990

Greenwood Press, 88 Post Road West, Westport, CT 06881
An imprint of Greenwood Publishing Group, Inc.

Printed in the United States of America

The paper used in this book complies with the
Permanent Paper Standard issued by the National
Information Standards Organization (Z39.48-1984).

10 9 8 7 6 5 4 3 2 1

A profound salute
to those who hesitate optimally and happily

Contents

1

Clarification

Again and again and again each of us, because we are human, asks the same questions: why do I hesitate, why should I hesitate? And variants occur: why did I hesitate, why should I have hesitated? The questions are asked not only about ourselves but also about other persons. We thus immediately show concern for two interrelated problems, the explanation and the morality of hesitation.

But what is hesitation? By definition hesitation shall refer to the time elapsing between the external or internal stimulation of an organism and his, her, or its internal or external response. The human being who appraises is the principal, the human being who witnesses the person's hesitation is the observer. The principal experiences the internal response and may arrive at a judgment or reach a decision before reacting externally; the observer views only the external response but may make inferences concerning the principal's internal response or questions him or her concerning that response. Since temporal intervals vary in duration, reference is made to degrees of hesitation.

Into that last paragraph the leading concepts to be employed in this book have been hurriedly packed. Let us catch our breath and explicate some of their meanings. Some time always elapses between stimulation and response. But does not a principal "immediately" blink when a bright light suddenly strikes his retina? Actually some time does elapse, a very brief fraction of a second, which can be measured by a sensitive instrument to be observed later either by the principal himself or an observer. Athletes and researchers concerned with the physiological bases of hesitation and behavior refer to brief hesitation as the reaction time or latency. Beyond phenomena such as eye-blinking or starting a race at the sound of a pistol, hesitation may extend from a few seconds or minutes to infinity. You hesitate to tell the waiter whether you wish fish or meat, you once hesitated years ago before selecting your best friend or your occupation. There are, then, degrees of hesitation.

Certainly principals may not be completely aware of all their internal responses as they hesitate: they do not or cannot monitor subliminal or unconscious processes that affect them. The speed with which individuals react to external stimulation and hence their degree of hesitation are influenced by their age, stress, gender, and fatigue over which they have little or no control.[1] The mode of measuring hesitation varies from the principal's subjective impression of a past, present, or future event, to the standardized calculation provided by a timer, stop watch, or calendar.

What happens to the principal between stimulation and response? Of course he senses or perceives whatever it is that stimulates him; otherwise the event passes him by and is not a source of stimulation. Whatever then takes place within him is his judgment or decision. The intervening responses, thoughts, or feelings that lead to the judgment or decision are of primary interest in our analysis of hesitation; thereafter attention is paid to possible actions, reactions, or overt behavior.

Explanation and Morality

With this verbal equipment we can reexamine and rephrase the question posed in the opening sentence in terms of explanation and morality. For explanation: how long do I hesitate and why? For morality: why should my hesitation be relatively short or long? Explanation and morality are usually inextricably linked to each other: we can explain what will happen, but should we allow it to happen?

The topic of explanation is obviously relevant when or if we seek to account for the milliseconds of delay between stimulation and response or for the decades of hesitation that pass until the poet feels prepared to publish his immortal poem. But why morality? A curious observer, perhaps an adventurous one, might try to explain why a principal of interest to him happens to have been at the precise place where he could see the light that caused his eyes to blink; and then, having very broad interests, that observer might decide that it was a good or a bad idea for the principal to have gone for the walk that eventually led to the bright light and his blinking. Good or bad presupposes a moral judgment. Another observer might conclude that the gods themselves induced him to walk and hence to blink. If you consider this eye-blinking episode trivial, then change the illustration to a country's leaders who must decide whether to improve, scrap, or use their nuclear weapons. How long do they hesitate and why? Should they hesitate and why?

The goal of explanation is to postulate the inevitability of a sequence of events that have occurred in the past or will occur in the future. Doctrines of inevitability are of two sorts.[2] The one usually labelled determinism characterizes science as well as any generalization based more or less solidly on experience. Deterministic doctrines themselves have no moral problems until the question is raised concerning their utilization. A particular fertilizer we know as a fact can stimulate and benefit a particular plant; but should we use it when we also know that it may have incidental and detrimental effects upon neighboring plants, animals, and human beings who advertently or inadvertently have contact with it?

The other explanatory doctrine is called by so many different names that I must use an awkward hyphenated label: fate-destiny. Here, as in religion, we have come to postulate a doctrine that stems not from rigorous experimental or empirical evidence but from our ancestors, our family, our peers, or our own subjective feelings, including our faith. "He who hesitates is lost:" do you subscribe to that principle or not (regardless of the degree of hesitation) and why? The double designation of fate-destiny seems necessary in the English language in order to differentiate between the approval and disapproval of the event that was, is, or will be the outcome. For destiny usually though not always refers to events securing approbation; fate usually, or at least more frequently, to events we prefer to avoid. It is our destiny to fall in love and we shall be married unless there is a fatal mishap.

Any explanation, whether invoking the doctrine of determinism or fate-destiny, has a temporal dimension. It may refer to factors that have operated in the past and that influence the present: background factors. Or the reference may be to the fleeting present and the pending future: foreground factors. Both background and foreground factors can be characterized in terms of variables associated with the situation at hand, the personality of the principal or principals, or both. Be patient (a form of hesitation): the utility of these distinctions will become clear in subsequent chapters.

It is self-evident that a principal and an observer may provide quite different explanations for the same behavior. Suppose an individual always hesitates a long while before coming to a decision and, as a result, fails to seize the moment that could enable him to achieve his own goals. He himself may suggest that his self-defeating behavior results from the complexity of his environment; an observer such as a psychiatrist may attribute this handicap to restraints placed upon him when he was young. One psychiatrist has drawn a useful distinction between illness and disease: illness refers to the patient's own conceptualization of his difficulties, disease to the characterization of the symptoms by a qualified or unqualified observer who relates them to some general theory applicable not only to this particular person but also to others having similar but not necessarily identical problems.[3] You think you know why you hesitate so long, I do too; which of us is "right"? The possible or probable discrepancy between the characterization and explanation provided by the principal and the observer constantly plagues or pleases us[4] and therefore receives here a special designation: variable linkage. We thus anticipate a mixture of understandings and misunderstandings between principals and observer and hence must be skeptical concerning the nature of any linkage.

The assumption of almost all explanatory doctrines is that we can intervene or can try to intervene to fulfill or not fulfill the dictates of the doctrine. Meteorologists may be able to forecast the weather and astronomers an eclipse, however, without being able to exercise control, but they can warn people concerning the probability of the event so that appropriate action may be taken. Otherwise scientists do plan their experiments and empirical observations and thus intervene. Similarly most religious doctrines indicate that, though human fate-destiny has been divinely predetermined in part or in whole by powers or a Power beyond human control, individuals must and can exercise restraint or obedience and thus ensure eventual salvation. A strong, compelling statement of our predicament reads:

Man through his awareness of the impact of the laws of social science on his values may intervene, in a way which is impossible in the natural sciences, to remove some of these laws from actual operation and to create new laws of social science. In this sense man can effect a factual change in the laws.[5]

Do you think, therefore, as a sociologist once proclaimed, that "the growth of knowledge is a disorderly movement"?[6] Not surprisingly immediate or ultimate explanations of hesitation also include instances ranging from those in which the principal allegedly cannot control them to those allegedly under his control.

Whenever—and I must add if ever—the principal has or seems to have no control over the degree of hesitation, a moral challenge is hardly relevant. The light shines, you blink your eyes, and that's that. Still, again, why did you look at the light? How long should you hesitate? The question is never simple when control is possible. For "should" may refer not only to one's ability to achieve an objective but also to morality. Elsewhere[7] I have convinced myself and perhaps a handful of others that morality may require that we consider more than the question of "should" or "ought" if all the reasons for moral decisions are to be both comprehended and utilized. The hypothetical principal asks himself, or provides conscious or unconscious answers to some or—rarely and miraculously—to all of the following questions:

1. *Motive*: what will I do?
2. *Potentiality*: what can I do?
3. *Rule and Duty*: what may or must I do?
4. *Anticipation*: what would or might be the consequences?
5. *Imperative*: what should, what ought I do?
6. *Intention*: what shall I do?
7. *Behavior*: what do or did I do?

The questions can be rephrased to refer to "we" when members of a group pass judgment and to "he," "she," or "they" when an observer judges one or more principals; and the tenses of the verbs can be changed to the various forms of the past and the future. Noteworthy is the fact that these questions concern all phases of the principal's knowledge, the past, present, and future.[8]

Almost identical questions are employed here to refer to the problems confronting the principal who hesitates under conditions when he judges or believes that a degree of hesitation is possible. Again the phrasing is arbitrarily in the first person and the present tense.

I hesitate because I know or do not know:

1. (*Motive*) what I will, wish, or need to do.
2. (*Potentiality*) how I can do it.
3. (*Rule and Duty*) whether I may or must do it.
4. (*Anticipation*) which consequences will result if I do it.
5. (*Imperative*) if I should do it.

6. (*Intention*) what I shall do now or in the future.

7. (*Behavior*) what I have previously done.

These questions of judgment become so relevant to the analysis of hesitation that they will be referred to subsequently and frequently as the Critical Questions. That blinking eye? Refer to Question 2 and above: he hesitates only during the short interval it takes for the reflex to occur; or if he expects to see the light, he may wish to try not to blink (Question 1), he may be able to delay the blink slightly. And a decision concerning the use of nuclear weapons? Perhaps its officials are emphasizing only the ultimate consequences for their nation by not "defending" themselves (Question 4).

For any one of the seven reasons associated with the Critical Questions, an explanatory principle must state, the principal hesitates, or from the observer's standpoint he may be said to hesitate, he may not know or he knows what he wants, he may think he can or cannot accomplish the objective, he may feel that what he wishes to do is or is not taboo, and so on. Also morally he may provide reasons for his failure to hesitate an appreciable length of time, which may not be true. He hesitated and decided not to contribute to that charity because obligations to his own family he considered more important: He was concerned with the needs of that family (personality as explanation to himself), and he also wondered whether its objectives were sensible (anticipation as moral judgment).

Judgments

It is insufficient merely to refer to degrees of hesitation, for then reference is made only to the time elapsing between stimulation and judgment or response and not to the presence or absence of replies to the Critical Questions during the temporal interval as judgments and decisions are made. Two processes must be distinguished. First, there is reflection: The consideration by the principal of one or more of those Questions with reference to the past or future; he does not know the answer to the questions or believes he has never previously responded to them. What would you do if you suddenly won a large sum of money in a lottery; how would you spend it not only immediately but over the months or years? What should parents do when their children wish to see a particular television program when they also think that exposure to such programs may eventually affect them adversely? The trite proverb glibly asserts that he who hesitates is lost, which is nonsense more often than not. The reflective person examines one or more of the Critical Questions, weighs the alternatives, and subsequently may or may not react in a manner that he, she, we, you, or other observers might call a better decision. The distinction between reflection and non-reflection is not clear-cut, just as it may not always be possible to distinguish between original and creative reflection. Yes, as one writer has suggested, anyone who proposes that "12 + 12 = 7,363,374" has demonstrated, if we accept conventional mathematical principles, his originality but not his creativity.[9] The example may or may not be convincing but some original theses—such as Galileo's concerning the rotation of the earth—at first glance may seem as unreflective and as uncreative as that mathematical equation. Perspective is essential. Reflection, so defined, may be slow or rapid; hence, a long period of hesitation is not necessarily accompanied by reflection.

The contrasting mode of hesitation is that of impulsivity (or impulsiveness, whichever you prefer) that is generally defined in terms of responding "without reflection," in contrast to being "deliberate"; hence, the principal fails "to stop and think before acting."[10] The individual acting on impulse is perhaps more likely to consider only the first Critical Question relating to his own goal and to slight the others, however relevant; thus you do not hesitate very long because you know what you will, wish, or need to do. Or you fail to consider one of the Questions that is crucial in a situation, you hesitate very briefly, you are impulsive because you do not anticipate the punishment that will ensue for yourself or for others. This conceptualization of impulsiveness is also in accord with conventional usage, such as the definition pro-

vided by a psychologist: "The tendency to act without stopping to think about the consequences; acting at the spur of
the moment."[11] Again, there is variable linkage since the
judgment of the principal and the observer may differ. The
observer is convinced that the principal was impulsive because he reacted quickly; but the principal knew it was not
necessary to pass judgment again, because he had reflected
sufficiently in the past concerning situations similar to the
one at the moment.

Reflection and impulsivity by these definitions differ in two
respects. Reflection considers more of the Critical Questions
than impulsivity; and reflection is usually but not always
less rapid than impulsivity. Both criteria are quantitative:
more or fewer Questions, slower or faster. Quantitative criteria suggest no sharp break between the phenomena. In the
present instance, therefore, reflection and impulsivity are at
the opposite ends of a continuum of hesitation and at some
point—or in some situations—merge, so that distinguishing
the two is always arbitrary and sometimes meaningless. A
quick response is not necessarily an impulsive one because,
as suggested in the next chapter, it may spring from reflection in the past.

Any temporal delay raises the challenge of reflection vs.
impulsivity. The deliberate delay in reaching a decision or
in carrying out an action, procrastination, may occur impulsively or after reflection. If impulsive, the principal may simply be blocked or lazy: he prefers not to reach a decision or
to react. If reflective, he may believe it necessary to delay in
order to weight possibilities or to acquire additional information.

A very tentative summary can be provided regarding these
two extremes of hesitation. Reflection occurs when the degree of hesitation is not brief, *or*, if brief, when the judgment
is based on a previous, relevant judgment involving the Critical Questions. In contrast, impulsivity occurs when the degree of hesitation is relatively brief *and* the judgment based
upon the perception of a previous, relevant judgment is superficial and involving few if any of the Critical Questions.
Admittedly this distinction between impulsivity and reflec-

tion is glib and will be refined later. Its very glibness, however, reflects normal usage and calls attention for the first time to the problem of relativity that continually plagues us.

Non-Apologia[12]

Whenever human beings are described, explained, or morally directed, the inescapable fact of variability appears. We can say, for example, that all—and now the variation—almost all persons seem to survive, but then we must immediately note the millions of ways in which they believe they can reach that often elusive objective. Think of the rich vocabularies that are employed to describe experience with internal and external strivings. "Strivings," why use such a word? Any glance about us is sufficient to point to some aspect of variability. A monk in Tibet, a philosopher in Paris, a mobster in Rome or in your neighborhood all have different ways of describing themselves and the different values they place upon their behavior.

If one wishes, the variability of non-human, even non-living matter can be similarly noted. Certainly there are differences when atoms or chemicals or rocks or rivers are compared, yet somehow progress in science has standardized the terminology to refer to the phenomena and indeed gradually to improve the theories describing or accounting for their variability. We find also impressive agreement among scientists concerning the critical variables to be examined and the ways in which their interrelationships are to be charted and then expressed. Do you employ a fate-destiny doctrine to explain whether it will snow in the north temperate zone in July or August?

Similar progress, similarly defined, is not to be noted among those researchers concerned with human behavior. Consider the so-called experts, psychiatrists, psychologists, and other social scientists. Certainly within the present century they have apparently uncovered new techniques to try to fathom human behavior; a reference to psychoanalysis, conditioning, or Rorschach blots points to the kind of innovation they have introduced and now utilize. But turmoil persists concerning the verbal apparatus and the theories to be employed to guide insight and research. Psychologists convince themselves and many bystanders that significant discoveries have been made when new words such as attribution, dissonance, or cognition appear in their journals and books and when the vocabulary simultaneously leads them along "new" paths and enables them to discover or probe "new" kinds of data.

Yes, progress in the behavioral sciences can be noted: "The great Western transcendental slide from God to Nature to Mind to Method was almost complete by the end of the nineteenth century, at least for the intellectual elite."[13] By concentrating upon method researchers are able to probe particular problems one at a time. We now know much more about discrete subjects such as honesty, helplessness, hunger, and hope—topics that begin with the letter "h", like hesitation. But our knowledge is piecemeal because each topic must be investigated more or less in isolation and under the assumption that "other things" remain equal. We know, in short, more about specific processes or events, yet the ultimate skeptical challenge remains: how do we put the pieces together again when we are dealing with the specific personality, group, or society? For this reason the subject of hesitation must be approached cautiously: we hesitate appreciably or not for countless reasons that may be noted one at a time, but cannot easily be assembled in a unified manner. The mere fact that the words hesitation, impulsivity, and reflection are in common speech means that the phenomena they denote are of interest to those who use them, yet their very utility warns us that they possess a variety of connotations and that they are ambiguous.

Rapid progress has been occurring within the last few decades in the strenuous efforts to find a physiological basis for human actions, to trace behavior to genes and to comprehend their constituents. The attributes of that progress are the use of the experimental method and precise mapping and quantification. In the present analysis, however, the physiological, anatomical, and biological approaches to the problem are excluded: the state of these disciplines would

require more space and speculation than seems desirable,
our priority remains strictly psychological, and the admittedly more basic topics have been treated adequately if tentatively in published works.[14] Likewise the relation of hesitation to drugs, though potentially important, is not only
complicated but also too uncertain to be considered in this
treatise. Illustrative is a review of the relevant literature by
a French scientist who has sought to investigate "whether
anxiety reduction or increased impulsivity is more likely to
account for . . . behavioral changes associated with decreased serotonergic transmission," that is, with a vasocon-
strictor in the blood stream. He also examines the effect of a
drug such as benzodiazepine that affects actions in all living
creatures. He concludes that "although selective serotonin
uptake blockers are increasingly used in clinical trials dealing with various forms of impulsivity (bulimia, alcoholism,
obsessive-compulsive disorders)," evidence for their effectiveness is lacking and therefore "the hypothesis of a crucial
link between serotonergic neurons and impulsive behavior
. . . still remains conjectural."[15] Seven qualified peers comment on that conclusion, but reach no consensus; therefore
the author himself finds no reason to change his view except
for minor details.[16]

Instead emphasis is placed upon experimental and empirical facts that produce generalizations and insights. Even on
this limited level apologies and reservations must be immediately expressed. First, it would be both erroneous and foolish to claim that all relevant studies have been either di-
gested or reported throughout these pages. The published
papers, reviews (some on an annual basis), and even books
are too numerous; before this sentence ends at least two new
articles will have appeared. An appendix summarizes trends
in 370 abstracts of articles relating to "impulsivity" that were
available during a nine-month period while this book was
being written. I cannot claim either to have read the original
articles that have been abstracted or even to have seen abstracts from previous or subsequent periods; and certainly
the flood will continue on and on. Merely attempting to assess the 370 articles mentioned in the appendix and, for ex-

ample, to explain or reconcile the contradictory findings that sometimes appear is beyond my patience and would require a boring, probably useless, tome in its own right.

What is one to do? I think we must retreat and skeptically admit that at the moment, perhaps forever, there can be no science of human judgment and behavior in the manner of the physical and many of the biological sciences. Knowledge about persons remains not cumulative in the rigorous sense of science but tentative. What we do perforce is to mention the highlights of what appears to be significant and compelling: we may be wrong, we may be right. Should we be skeptical about our skepticism?

One must also claim that it is impossible to offer generalizations that have not previously been made in some form. Whenever one wishes, it is possible to find in Aristotle, Socrates, and Plato some trace of what appears now to be a new insight. Why, then, go on? We go on for two reasons. Whatever new information we have can be incorporated into the generalizations. And whether or not we realize our advantages, we have absorbed some of the wisdom of the ages and have attempted to express that wisdom in a manner that can be comprehended and utilized in our time. The goal is to view each problem in broad perspective, even a new one, that is adapted to our time and what we believe to be our particular insights.

Current research, including the experimental and empirical that will be cited, merits criticisms from many standpoints, and indeed volumes grace library shelves that do just that.[17] American and other psychologists find it understandably convenient to use students as subjects in their research. These individuals are easily available or they can be compelled to "volunteer" for a small amount of money or to discharge an obligation of the course in which they are enrolled. They generally are eager to cooperate with their instructor, especially when they are genuinely convinced that they are thereby advancing "science." Young men and women—and perforce they usually are young—surely are not representative of the human species and therefore the generalizations drawn from the experiments or empirical data

may well be limited to them, to the Zeitgeist in which they
have been socialized and are now active, and to many of their
demographic attributes. In addition, the outcome of experiments in social psychology may depend on whether the variable of interest has been manipulated realistically or by means
of a contrived scenario to which the subjects are asked to
react as if the situation were real; and the subjects themselves may be of a particular gender and, of course, are residents in a particular country.[18]

Some of these methodological charges can and should be
levelled against the most creative investigator of them all,
Freud. As has been said many times, he perforce was dependent upon the atypical sample of Viennese patients who
formed the basis for his productive theory concerning the
role of unconscious factors in human affairs. Come, come,
what right have I to pay this banal, critical tribute to Freud?
For I am also embedded in my particular milieu from which
I cannot escape and, therefore, cannot hope to transcend my
own inevitable limitation. Yes, 'tis true, of course, I have not
mastered all the studies and all the thoughts that might be
related to the topic of hesitation; of course I exercise conscious and unconscious bias in selecting the illustrations I
employ; of course my knowledge, and yours, is imperfect. I
take sensible refuge in the conviction that any datum or any
thought—even when conventionally derived—points to some
sort of guide to assist us in the intellectual wilderness in which
we dwell.

What I have been able to do is to select from published
studies those which, in my fallible opinion, offer significant
understanding or at least illustrate a problem or a difficulty.
It is comforting to have a generalization replicated in another investigation, yet there is always the possibility that a
single study all by itself provides the insight we seek; sometimes a flash is more illuminating than a series of lesser lights.
In addition I provide four safeguards to avoid going too far
astray:

1. Whenever specific data suffer from the limitations I have
been mentioning, I shall alert myself and you by using the
word *conventional* which hereafter will be employed as a

substitute for "a sample of American students (i. e., from Canada or the United States) who were the subjects of an experimental or empirical investigation usually in an artificial situation contrived by the investigator."

2. Also to emphasize the limited generalizability of a study the adverb *once* will be inserted into the summary of the research. Like other social scientists, I shall also preface some verbs with the auxiliary "may" and thus indicate that "things often don't turn out the same way twice."[19] More often than not the verbs in this context are in the past tense in order to avoid the omniscient impression the present tense can create.

3. References to authors and their works are honored and acknowledged only in footnotes that are segregated at the end of this volume. The symbol "cf." before a note suggests that the information to which it refers is considered only tentative or has served the function of giving rise to what is stated in the text; the author or authors are thus absolved from the responsibility for the statement. Many of the "cf." authors may be surprised by their appearance in the context where reference is made to them.

4. Since I often can provide only a tentative impression from the research jungle, I shall call upon you, the adventurous reader, for assistance. For you know when you yourself and other persons are hesitating; I address you directly and appeal to you to decide. I am not resorting to a literary device; I am asking you to provide your own data. Throughout this book, as must be already evident in the preceding pages, rhetorical questions are addressed to anonymous readers in the second person; they are only raised and then left unanswered. Why? Not only do I hesitate to provide the answers, but I would also thus enlist the cooperation of the reader who is thereby challenged to participate in this enterprise. You are the audience, and you are wise and consequently skeptical.

I admit, unashamedly, a bias in this analysis of hesitation: greater emphasis is placed upon the subjective ways in which principals experience and are conscious of events than upon the objective data provided by observers. Why? Any philos-

opher or ordinary person would call that question superfluous since the answer ought to be obvious. Some psychologists, however, cling to the view that insight into behavior
can be secured only by studying the stimuli that have impact upon us and the responses we then make; what happens
in the black box, in inaccessible consciousness, is too subjective and can be dismissed simply by postulating whatever
occurs between the stimulus and the response as an intervening variable. But others would agree with a view once
expressed by a psychologist: "The most primitive and fundamental reason for the study of experiential events remains
the most compelling—the personal conviction of humans
[human beings!], probably including most psychologists, that
direct experience occurs and is in some sense a real, integral,
and most significant property of the perceptual-behavioral
event."[20] Or assent can be obtained perhaps for another bit
of truth and wishful thinking: "Through his higher cognitive
functions, the human individual is equipped with especially
efficient means for designing the behavioral ways toward the
satisfaction of his needs.[21] Yes, of course, when one thinks of
medicine, literature, and airplanes; no, when one thinks of
wars, poverty, and evils like dishonesty and selfishness.

I return to the original and unoriginal questions that opened
this chapter: Why do I hesitate, why should I hesitate? With
our conceptual apparatus, the task ahead can be quickly out-
lined. First, however uninspiring, it is absolutely essential to
suggest and evaluate the methods that have been employed
to measure or assess hesitation (chapter 2). Then principals
must be located in their society which has a unique culture
concerning degrees of hesitation (chapter 3). We realize that
each person is somewhat unique and hence we must consider the uniquenesses of personality and the ways they hesitate (chapter 4). Next, even when we know or believe we
know the culture of principals and their individual attributes, we must examine the effects persons have on one another's degree of hesitation (chapter 5) as well as the effects
of specific situations on their judgments and behavior (chapter 6). In conclusion, we confront a practical and moral
question: under what circumstances are degrees of hesita-

tion necessary or desirable (chapter 7), and how can the necessary and desirable degree be cultivated (chapter 8)?

And now this introductory, clarifying, definition-ridden chapter will end, as will all succeeding chapters, with a brief benediction.

IN SHORT: above a whisper let it be proclaimed that comprehending hesitation can provide a significant universal insight into human awareness and behavior; whatever we do or observe others doing occurs in a temporal frame of reference and hence requires some degree of hesitation.

2

Routes and Measurement

In order to find a route through the jungle of meanings cluttering hesitation and its methods of measurement, it may be helpful for a moment to utilize three symbols to serve as guides:

0: zero or unknown effect of past judgment upon the present judgment

H−: hesitation inclining toward impulsivity

H+: hesitation inclining toward reflection

"0" means that the influence of the past (background factors) is believed or assumed by the principal or observer to be absent or negligible. You have never met that person before and therefore his actions in the past do not affect your present judgment of him. The symbols of "H−" and "H+" refer only to the ends of the continuum of hesitation: clearly hesitation must be operationally defined as impulsivity merges into reflection. Unless there has been 0, the foreground factor must be negligible (H−) or influential (H+).

With these three symbols, six routes emerge:

Route	Past	Present
1a	0	H −
1b	0	H +
2a	H −	H −
2b	H −	H +
3a	H +	H −
3b	H +	H +

Since unobtrusive reference on occasion but only rarely will be made to this schema, the designating symbols are both consistent and few in number: the arabic numerals refer to hesitation *in the past* (1 to zero or unknown hesitation, 2 to inclination toward impulsivity, and 3 to inclination toward reflection); and the letters refer to hesitation *in the present* (a to impulsivity and b to reflection). As ever, the principal and the observer may be convinced that an action has emerged from different routes (variable linkage). You quickly snub another person because you know that you have had an unfavorable experience with him, and have determined to avoid him forever after (Route 2a); but, the person, the wretch being snubbed, has not known about these experiences or has interpreted them differently, hence he thinks you are reacting impulsively (Route 1a). Clearly you have access to your past judgments, but he can only observe the snub and the speed with which you react. You and he are using different methods to assess the hesitation whose temporal latency is close to zero. Methods, therefore, influence routes; they must be tediously explored. But do note in advance the following appropriate comment by one who has toiled in the vineyard of hesitation: "If the clinical use of impulsivity is confusing, the range of techniques for measuring it is even more confusing."[1] Little wonder that the state of this art is a trifle disorderly and tentative.[2]

Matching

The most widely used and justly acclaimed method employed by psychologists and other systematic investigators is known as the "Matching Familiar Figures Test" which will be called here, to emphasize its obvious feature, simply the Matching Test and which will be discussed at some length because it reveals measurement problems shared by other methods. The test was designed originally by an American,[3] and has been used somewhat extensively in other countries. Most of the principals have been children, but in a slightly modified form it has also assessed the hesitancy of adolescents and adults. At the top of a card the subject is shown a drawing of a familiar object, the "standard," below which are from four to eight (frequently six) "similar variants, only one of which is completely identical to the standard." Twelve or fewer cards with other objects thus displayed are then offered one after the other and judged. On one of the cards, for example, the subject sees a teddy bear sitting in a chair; in all six of the variants, the bottom of the chairs are identical, but the position of the animal's head, hands, and tie as well as the shape of his feet vary slightly. Another card displays a tree, the branches and leaves on which differ minutely in the variants. After making his choice, the subject may be only encouraged without being told whether he has selected the correct variant before he is shown the next card; or, if incorrect, he may be asked to try again. The same procedure is followed as each of the cards is displayed.

Two scores relating to hesitation can be obtained from this test: the mean time it takes the individual to select what he believes to be the correct variant on each card and the mean number of correct choices. These two measures, latency and accuracy, are frequently negatively related to each other; at least among American and other children there has been a tendency for those responding quickly to commit a larger number of errors. The obtained correlations, however, have been far from perfect and therefore one cannot be substituted for the other as a measure of hesitation. What is usually done[4] is to locate the median of each of the two measures and then to combine the two into four groups above and below the median which may be then labelled as follows to place the individuals being examined in a single category.

Label	latency	accuracy
impulsive	below	below
reflective	above	above
fast, accurate	below	above
slow, inaccurate	above	below

After being classified, subjects perform either immediately or later in order to determine the relation between the Matching Test scores and other behavior; or that test is repeated later to determine their consistency over time.

The test has been respectfully criticized.[5] Originally too many of the correct variants on each card were located in the first row of three, not the second; its reliability (i. e., the relation of the scores on the cards to one another or the immediate or short-range stability of the total scores) has been questioned and not adequately demonstrated; and the stability of the measure over longer periods of time has been shown to be far from perfect. More important, often only two of the groups, the impulsives and the reflectives, have been considered, with the remaining two being neglected. But you wouldn't call a person impulsive who responds quickly and correctly to a question or a problem, would you? Consider, for example, two groups of ten-year old Mexican children, one retarded and one normal, who were once given the Matching Test. They did not differ when they were divided on the basis of fast-inaccurate vs. slow-accurate, but they did differ when the division was between fast-accurate (efficient) vs. slow-inaccurate (inefficient).[6] This latter division derived from the same test may also produce significant differences among children on quite different kinds of tasks. Among subjects responding quickly, even finer discriminations have been made: the accurate, the adaptive (few errors), and the maladaptive (many errors).[7] Impulsivity has also been defined, on a slightly modified version of the Matching Test, to refer to those who are slow and inaccurate.[8]

Another solution to this problem of classification involves a consideration of the background factor in categorizing the principal's reaction to this test or in any situation: is the background 0 in a relative sense, H−, or H+? When this is done, the usual procedure of scoring the test is clearly ahistorical and not historical: it is assumed that Route 1a characterizes impulsivity and Route 1b reflection. But there are alternatives:

Impulsive when the principal does not reflect in the present and has not hesitated at all or only slightly concerning the problem at hand (Routes 1a and 2a)

Reflective when the principal: First, reflects in the present and has not or scarcely hesitated in the past (Routes 1b or 2b) or has also reflected in the past (Route 3b), and second, does not reflect in the present but has hesitated or reflected in the past (Route 3a)

Those categories now listed serve to alert the reader to the need to know in some detail how each method categorizes the principal.

Another defect of the Matching Test springs from its laudable objectivity. Perforce it provides no insight into the judgmental processes resulting in the selection of the variants. According to a Swiss psychologist, principals differ significantly in this respect, and hence it would be desirable to know how much time during hesitation is devoted to encoding and making inferences concerning the event, to applying these judgments to the problem at hand, and to responding.[9] The objective measure of latency does not reveal whether the choice of the variant by the principal stems from a judgment based on despair or on reasoned selection.[10] In different words, elapsed time is a component of hesitation, but what of the replies to the Critical Questions during the delay? With an objective approach we know nothing more than the outcome of the reflection that has or has not occurred during the elapsed time; we do not know which intervening Critical Questions, if any, have been asked by the principal and what his replies have been. The originator of the test has noted the extent to which subjects glance at the variants,[11] and at least one investigator has attempted to come even a bit closer to the judgmental processes without abandoning objectivity: she employed a special "eye-marker camera" that enabled her to record the extent and frequency with which the subject glanced at the alternative variants before responding.[12]

Advocates and users of the Matching Test invoke ready and somewhat impressive defenses. Dividing a group of subjects on the basis of those above and below the median with respect to latency and errors provides norms within the particular group and thus avoids irrelevant standards from other groups. The very objectivity of the test within limits is methodologically desirable. Subjective elements are controlled: supposedly the principal can be put at ease, and the experimenter or the person administering the test can be carefully selected and trained to gain rapport with the subject without affecting his or her judgments. Detailed knowledge concerning the processes of reflection need not be known when only the outcome is of interest. Background factors in the past constitute a research problem and, hence, need not be provided as the test is administered.

A final criticism of the Matching Test is applicable perhaps to almost all measuring devices: the testing situation is artificial and, hence, usually not representative of real-life situations in which hesitation plays a role. It is not, as two reviewers of the experimental literature have remarked, "an ecologically natural environment."[13] The situation created by the test is "too narrow to deal with everyday behavior."[14] The child or the adult is confronted with a new situation, one with which presumably he has had no previous experience, and is suddenly asked to identify a similar variant; for him this experimental situation has been structured. The originator of the test as well as his friendly and unfriendly critics constantly indicate that hesitation is thus being assessed under conditions of "uncertainty": the subject is uncertain concerning which of the teddy bears exactly matches the standard at the top of the card. It is encouraging to note the high relationship once established among kindergarten children between their classification based on the test and seven other verbal tests also measuring uncertainty (e.g., the hesitation in responding to questions such as "What is a nail?").[15] Certainly such uncertainty does occur in "real" life but not always. As a pedestrian you hesitate only a fraction of a second when a speeding car approaches you; you are not uncertain concerning the objective of safety you would attain. Do these shoes you are trying on in a shop feel comfortable? The uncertainty here is again limited to an objective you can appreciate, but you may never know whether you have selected the equivalent of the correct teddy bear. Maybe the pair you rejected would have turned out to be more comfortable. The assumption of the experimenter or clinician who administers the test, moreover, may be that the principal's behavior in the matching situation resembles a general tendency, just as any intelligence test offers novel challenges on the basis of which a disposition is presumably tapped; and the assumption concerning both tendencies may or may not be valid. In other situations, perhaps more often in real life, the principal is confronted with situations that not only recur but also therefore enable him to come to a decision on the basis of his past experience (Routes 2a, 3a). Such experience is difficult to acquire during the Matching Test. As he perceives successive cards and must select a variant, the subject may learn how to approach each successive challenge, but he cannot easily profit from these ongoing experiences because he usually is not told whether his selections of variants on previous cards have been correct or incorrect. In a series of experiments with American students whose impulsivity was determined by self-reports on a questionnaire, it was once shown that providing bonuses (actually money) when they correctly selected the correct matchings during a limited period of time revealed no difference between the impulsive and reflective subjects during the early phase of the experiment; then later they apparently judged whether it would be more rewarding to be fast and inaccurate or slow and accurate: which method would produce the greater net gain?[16] A similar tradeoff between speed and accuracy was once demonstrated among children between the ages of three and four as their impulsivity was assessed by means of a controlled exercise similar to the Matching Test and designated by the snappy acronym KRISP (Kansas Reflection-Impulsivity Scale for Pre-schoolers).[17]

Probing

Other methods somewhat resembling the Matching Test have been employed to observe and record their behavior as subjects respond to standardized tests. Quite typical is the comparison that was once made between two groups of American adolescents, one hospitalized for psychiatric reasons and the other normal. They were given two tests: they were asked to draw a person and also to locate a simple figure embedded in a more complex one. Both situations produced operationalized measures of impulsivity as assessed by recording the latency of their reaction and their errors. Incidentally, the two tasks yielded related measures of impulsivity which in turn tended to be related to ratings of impulsivity by psychiatric nurses or teachers as well as to scores on the Matching Test.[18] An Israeli investigator attempted—unsuccessfully, it seems—to distinguish the impulsivity of "young offenders" and controls by having his subjects trace a circle as slowly as possible.[19] Standard techniques of psychologists have interpreted or measured hesitation; for example, the Thematic Apperception Test (a projective device that taps a person's dispositions by having him view a series of pictures and then relate stories based on them) can be scored in terms of the quantity and quality of the aggressive actions that are portrayed, and it is then assumed that impulsive principals tend to display more aggression than those who are allegedly reflective.[20]

Questioning

Why not simply ask a principal whether he considers himself impulsive or reflective; or why not pose a similar question concerning that principal to an observer? The two words slip easily into our vocabulary so that a reply to either question can usually be anticipated without reflection. Systematic investigation, however, requires a series of subtler questions before classifying the individual. An analogy: are you a liberal or conservative? I am unable to contrive an objective situation in which your behavior demonstrates to me your political conviction. What I do is ask you on a printed questionnaire or in an interview a series of questions about your philosophy concerning government, your attitudes toward political officials or their decisions, the candidate for whom you have voted in the past and intend to vote for in the future, even perhaps the ways in which you claim you treat your family and other human beings. I then tabulate your verbal replies, compare them with other persons' replies, and finally through statistical manipulation arrive at a conclusion that places you decidedly or weakly in one camp rather than the other. A similar technique has been employed with reference to hesitation and consequently is able to provide the kind of background information that the Matching Test as such fails to obtain.

In the West perhaps the most popular and fruitful series of questionnaires has been devised by a British psychologist and his colleagues. After elaborate analyses of questionnaires they themselves and others have decided that what they call "impulsiveness" consists of four factors which will be discussed in chapter 3 but which are listed here to illustrate the kinds of questions that can be asked by means of this approach:

1. *Narrow impulsiveness*: "Do you mostly speak before thinking things out?"; "Before making up your mind, do you carefully consider all the advantages and disadvantages?"

2. *Risk-taking*: "Would life with no danger be too dull for you?"; "When on a holiday, do you look for relaxation rather than excitement?"

3. *Non-planning*: "Do you like planning things well ahead of time?"; "When buying things, do you usually bother about the guarantee?"

4. *Liveliness*: "Do you prefer to 'sleep on it' before making decisions?"; "Can you put your words into thoughts quickly?"[21]

The same kind of information can be obtained with items that are slightly differently worded (for example, the first item above can become "I usually think before I act")[22] and the statistical analysis among other principals, as in Sweden, produces different components[23] from the four just listed above.

Clearly this method deals with more significant aspects of the judgments and actions that involve hesitation than the method of asking principals which of the drawings of six teddy bears resembles the standard atop the sheet. Let us sidestep the criticism of ethnocentrism that can be hurled at the questionnaire which is designed for persons in the United Kingdom and also less frequently in North America. Instead we can concentrate briefly upon two problems. The first is that of validity: can or will the respondents tell the truth about their own judgments? We know only too well that publicly expressed attitudes frequently differ from those receiving private approval.[24] That question about truth is unanswerable if we examine only the responses on the questionnaire itself, and, so, an instrument like the Matching Test has the advantage of providing factual information about principals in a limited situation. In administering a questionnaire, the investigator seeks to have the principal at least feel at ease: he himself is friendly or neutral. He may promise to keep the replies confidential or indicates that the replies will be anonymous. Data from such a questionnaire, whether valid or not, at least provide information concerning how principals view or purport to view themselves with respect to hesitation. The only satisfactory solution to this problem of validity is to try to determine whether or not there is a relation between the scores it yields and some other criterion such as a behavioral measure or the individuals' reputation with respect to hesitation.

A second problem is that of reliability: whether or not the principal is telling the truth about himself; are his replies to the questions dependent upon his momentary mood or upon some relatively stable disposition? Some safeguards are possible, in addition to those concerned with validity. The relations of the items on the questionnaire to one another (how each correlates with the total score or how the odd-numbered items correlate with the even-numbered ones) can provide one measure of immediate consistency not only of the principal but also of the questionnaire itself; the correlation of the four hesitation factors mentioned above tended without exception to be low. Another measure is obtainable by repeating the identical or a very similar questionnaire more than once: do respondents receive approximately the same scores? Either method, however, is fallible. Consistency ascertained statistically can be misleading: the hesitation of a given individual may fluctuate with the different items tapped in the questionnaire and over time as a result of changes in mood or experience.

Sometimes it is not possible to determine the validity or the reliability when questionnaire or interview findings are interpreted. In a sample of British families there was once a slight tendency for parents to rate themselves as well as their twin children somewhat similarly with respect to impulsivity on a questionnaire.[25] Do these alleged similarities mean that impulsivity has genetic roots like hair color or that social psychological climate may be cultivated that affects choice of spouses and is transmitted to twins; or did the respondents share a stereotype concerning hesitation that they projected upon each other and their children?

A warning: often a verbal response to a written or spoken question cannot be interpreted as an instance of impulsivity or reflection. Chinese students were once asked to check off on a printed list, both before and after taking an examination, the common excuses they "believed might account" for their performance; they ranged from "I did not study enough" and "I did not have enough time to study" to "Lectures were too difficult" and "I'm too tense and nervous." In this situation it might be argued that their replies were spontaneous and impulsive or that they were a function of prior reflection that became salient as a result of the investigator's question. The fact that their excuses before or after the examination had little or no relation to their actual performance is interesting, but does not settle the issue at hand.[26] If the students had been questioned orally, their reaction time to the question might have provided a clue, but even a quick response could have been either impulsive or a function of previous reflection (Routes 1a or 3a). Similarly, can the time it takes to express an attitude in response to a question indicate the degree of hesitation? Generally attitude strength itself can be ascertained by the length of the interval before the principal responds: the shorter the time, the stronger the attitude. It is probable, however, that the reaction time and the attitude strength also depend upon the individual's direct experience with the referent of the attitude and the number of times the attitude has been previously expressed; in addition, the presence of its referent also shortens the time.[27] What may appear to be an impulsive action, consequently, depends upon a combination of factors, some of which required reflection in the past.

Questionnaires and interviews, being designed not for animals but for human beings, can produce what in natural sciences is called the Heisenberg or uncertainty principle: The act of measuring may affect what is being measured. When principals fill out a questionnaire or respond to an interviewer, they may learn something about themselves either from the act of answering the questions or, if it is made available to them, from the resulting score or diagnosis they receive from the investigator. Have you ever considered, if I may mention one item from the risk-taking scale above, whether "life with no danger [would] be too dull for you?" Such insight or pseudo-insight into yourself may subsequently influence your judgments and actions. This contaminating factor is probably less frequent in connection with the Matching Test when the subjects are not told how well or how poorly they are performing or have performed; but even then the very challenge of being tested by an adult investigator or, if they are given information about their performance, their inability to locate the correct teddy bear et seq. might damage a sensitive ego and thereafter affect his tendency to hesitate.

Questioning assumes a different form when one or more observers provide information concerning the principal's impulsivity and reflection or behavior related thereto. The observers may be the principal's parents, his peers, or other "knowledgeable informants."[28] Similar doubts must be raised concerning such information: are the observations valid and reliable? In addition, it is vital to know, when more than one source is tapped, whether the individuals agree with one another. And then the omnipresent challenge of the variable linkage: should we believe the principal or the reporters?

In passing and as quickly as possible it seems appropriate here to mention a statistical method, that of factor analysis, that has been employed especially frequently in connection with questionnaires. What the investigators did when they specified the four factors comprising impulsiveness—narrow impulsiveness, risk-taking, non-planning, and liveliness—mentioned in this section was first to determine the significant statistical relations (or correlations) among the items on the questionnaires. Four groupings emerged in which those relations were impressive and to which they then attached the labels. Instead of utilizing only items from questionnaires, other kinds of information can be similarly interrelated. In one study, for example, data from the Matching Test, self-reports, estimation and production of temporal interval, and simple reaction times were statistically manipulated and the three emerging factors were labelled: spontaneous, not persistent, and carefree impulsivity.[29] Obviously the choice of labels for the factors in these studies is arbitrary and therefore consensus among investigators is difficult or impossible to discern.

Indices

For many reasons people in every society keep records of human activities in archives and their equivalent or in oral traditions that have originated before the lifetime of the current generation and that persist long afterwards. Data of this kind can be utilized as indices of hesitation. The records of 230 young American males who had been convicted of rape or child molestation, for example, were once later examined by two sociologists. Available were clinical files, prison records, and observations by officials. There emerged from the analysis three behavioral domains that could be interpreted as indicating impulsivity: the amount of "planning and forethought" in connection with the criminal act (which varied from planning partially or in detail to responding after en-

countering the victim); "a general life style of impulsive behavior" (which included past behavior such as unstable employment history and aimlessness or failure to settle down);
and "transiency" (morbidity, aimlessness, and seclusive-
ness).[30] Panics of any kind, such as a selling wave on a stock
market, or crazes for a style of clothing or of speaking can
be subsequently interpreted as symptoms of impulsivity—
maybe so.

Observation

Any observer who has an opportunity actually to observe
a single principal or a group of principals once or over a
period of time is likely to be able to answer questions concerning his or their degree of hesitation. The observation may
be deliberate as when a coach notes that a runner has learned
to respond "instantly" to the gun sound that begins the race,
when a psychiatrist treats his patient, or when an investigator decides to observe subjects through a one-way vision
screen. Or the observation can be retrospective: an investigator requests parents or schoolteachers to rate, respectively, their own children or their pupils on a scale or its
equivalent that he provides.

Let psychiatry highlight the problems of this method. One
psychiatrist believes that neurotic style consists of "an impairment of normal feelings of deliberateness and intention."
The patient succumbs to an urge that later meets with his
disapproval: "I just *did* it—I don't know why."[31] Perhaps it
is unlikely that other psychiatrists would agree with this
symptom of impulsivity; even the very general concept of
impairment may not be employed by members of the profession. In Britain, for example, a small sample of practicing
psychiatrists was once confronted with a standardized definition of "impulsivity or unpredictability", applicable to "at
least two areas which are potentially self-damaging, e.g.,
spending, sex, gambling, drug or alcohol abuse, shoplifting,
overeating, physically self-damaging acts." Some, but by no
means all, found this conception useful in differentiating between so-called borderline patients and others not con-

sidered in that category or psychotic.[32] The relation between a psychiatrist and patient, moreover, is private, so that both practically and ethically there is no objective way to assess the validity and reliability of the subjective observation.

All the methods examined thus far, including the present one, assess the individual principal or a specified group of individuals. Like the psychiatrist's patient, it is an individual who is called upon to match the standard teddy bear, to find the solution to some problem, or to reply to a question or a series of questions; it is individuals whose actions in the past have contributed to the data being employed as an index. With some perspectives and in many scholarly disciplines, hesitation is assessed by combining observation with inference or knowledge. When a spectator at a track meet observes that the race begins after the starter's pistol is heard, he does not conclude that the runners are acting impulsively (Route 1a); unless he has arrived from Mars he knows that the runners have trained themselves to start running as quickly as possible when they hear the sound, they are not impulsive (Route 3a). A historian or a sociologist does not observe all the persons who have participated in events in order to draw conclusions concerning the customs, the culture, or even the modal value regarding some aspect of hesitation. If you speedily avoid the number thirteen or are thrilled whenever you see your country's flag, you and I know you are again giving expression to what you have been taught long ago. An anthropologist who describes a society has not in all probability observed every person in that society; rather he has lived among the people, has listened and talked and observed only some of them; his description he believes applies to all the principals except for the aberrant ones, only a few of whom he has likewise observed.

Chaos?

Without doubt hesitation hunters have been mightily ingenious in devising methods to assess the phenomenon of interest to themselves and to us. We must now pause and wonder how we can proceed in our analysis and exposition.

It is clear that no one method is to be preferred once and for all, the way the centigrade scale has standardized the measuring of temperature in an objective sense. Even the Matching Test itself has variants. It is necessary to inquire whether any one of the methods examined in this chapter yields a true or valid measure of hesitation. Usually the criterion is a formal or informal rating by the individual's peer or peers: do they agree with his own rating of himself or the deduction that is made from a sample of his behavior? But then, as a result of the variable linkage, we must wonder whose judgment to accept, that of the principal who knows himself and who has observed himself again and again and again? But does he know himself? What about his unconscious? What about self-deception? Similar skepticism can be expressed concerning peer ratings, even when—as indicated above— the reliability and interrelationship of their ratings are determined to be high. Since principals are human beings, the same challenge arises in connection with many of their other propensities, but the conclusion to be drawn is absolutely, yes absolutely clear-cut: any characterization of hesitation is subject to error and must be accepted with steady, reserved skepticism.

There is no easy solution to this chaos in the domain of measurement. Yes, one can measure precisely reaction time or any temporal interval between stimulation and response, but that index is too crude because it neglects judgmental responses as well as background factors. Or one might expect that different methods of measuring hesitation are related to one another and hence that it matters little which method one employs. Yes, scores on the Matching Test by thirty hospitalized adolescents have been found to be impressively but not perfectly related to ratings provided by three psychiatric nurses as well as to their actual behavior observed in the clinic.[33] On the other hand, the scores on the same test by grade-school children whose teachers had identified them as being impulsive or lacking self-control were either unrelated or poorly related to their scores on a self-control inventory; their latency scores on that test were unrelated or scarcely related to ratings by the teachers and

parents and even by themselves.[34] With such a negative outcome and with even high correlations that are less than perfect, the sad conclusion must be drawn that one method of
assessing hesitation cannot be substituted for another or that
hesitating human beings are too complex or varied to be
captured once and forever by a single measurement.

In the light of this methodological situation all we poor
mortals can do is always, even when it seems impossible, to
operationalize and define our measures of hesitation. It is
both tempting and easy to refer to reflective and impulsive
principals, but to avoid ambiguity and confusion we must
first know how they received the designation. At the risk of
being pedantic, as already threatened, I shall sometimes refer to the six routes being followed in a discussion or analysis and I shall mention the method being followed on these
routes. At the very least we can then reduce the chaos slightly
by being cautious, tentative, and skeptical.

*IN SHORT: deterministically, it must be said, a temporal interval
elapses between stimulation and the ensuing action; instruments
may be useful to measure the elapsed time, but they do not readily
reveal, if at all, the precise nature of the psychological processes
intervening between stimulation and the judgment or decision;
modes of assessing degrees of hesitation within personalities are
available, but their validity must be cautiously evaluated.*

3

Culture and Society

One foundation for human judgments and behavior is to be found in culture and society. For hesitation, that foundation is broad and not always specific. Sneezing occurs in every society when nerve endings in the nose are irritated; but cultural elements may determine whether the reflex is repressed or directed away or toward bystanders, the reaction of those bystanders, and the interpretation placed upon the audible explosion. The ability of athletes and warriors to react quickly must be traced in part to genetic factors which then are encouraged to develop within a society. Otherwise cultural and societal factors provide the setting for hesitation, particularly with reference to regulating behavior; they are the powerful background factors. A bit poetically and hence perhaps validly one anthropologist has exclaimed that human beings are "incomplete or unfinished animals who complete or finish [themselves] through culture—and not through culture in general but through particular forms of it."[1]

Culturally or societally determined experience in the past affects hesitation in the present (H− or H+ via Routes 2a, 2b, 3a, or 3b; not 0 via Route 1a or 1b), even when observers must only speculate concerning how and why the effect has

been achieved. High school students in India once formed
anagrams, some of which were easy and others difficult to
compose. They were then asked to account for their performance. Almost all of them attributed successes to internal
factors, namely, their own effort and their ability. Those reporting they had been living an existence with few deprivations may have been protecting their egos because they tended
to attribute their failures to bad luck and other external factors; in contrast, those reporting that they had been living a
deprived existence tended also to attribute their failures to
themselves by referring to their own low ability and less effort.[2] Presumably, the investigators say in effect, the seri-
ously deprived were less able to distinguish between external and subjective sources of their successes and failures in
forming anagrams because generally they had been receiving too little gratification in their society.

Rules and Duties

We can begin on a lofty note: "All the world's a stage / And
all the men and women merely players / They have their ex-
its and their entrances / And one man in his time plays many
parts." Our guide Shakespeare is thus pointing out,[3] a bit
earlier than modern sociologists made the same observation,
that principals continually play different roles—he specifies
"seven"—as they pass from infancy to senility. We know also
that the infant may be "mewling and puking in the nurse's
arm" but that, since he or she mewls and pukes somewhat
distinctively, we must also consider the infant a distinctive
human being. In addition the nurse may or may not be the
mother who has varied convictions concerning how to com-
fort the child or to prevent the outbursts in the first place.
"Then the whining school-boy, with his satchel / And shining
morning face, creeping like a snail / Unwillingly to school."
Again, as is true of the remaining five stages, we can raise
unpoetic questions concerning the variability of the generalization: some girls as well as boys may be eager to reach
school; many traditional societies have never had schools in

a formal sense, though all of them must socialize their willing or unwilling youngsters.

At any moment principals beyond the stage of infancy appreciate the existence of rules they must follow and the duties they must peform. Shakespeare's schoolboy was English; if he had been a Zulu at the time, his rules, duties, and hence his life's stages would have been quite different. Immediately, however, note must be taken not only of the variability of rules and duties from society to society but also of their variability within each society. Without resorting to a neologism we can observe that some of these rules and duties are mandatory, others elective. Any normal schoolboy has already learned the language of his parents or his nurse: he has had no choice, acquiring the prevailing language is mandatory. His parents know they must clothe him, but they themselves select the precise clothes in a Western society at least, even as indeed they may reject some fate-destiny in favor of deterministic explanations or switch to another political party: within limits, some cultural traits here are elective. The individual recognizes this distinction as the "degrees of freedom" he possesses as a principal for himself or as an observer for another person; a child has less freedom in school than he does at home.[4]

I hesitate a moment or more because I do not know whether I may or must do it; I do not hesitate because I know that I may or must do it. Rules and regulations in a society as well as the prescribed duties tend to produce mandatory rather than elective responses to the Critical Questions relevant to pending events. Then principals need not hesitate for long, they have already reflected, they know what they are supposed to do or not do (Route 3a). You do not impulsively kill another person, damnably annoying or frustrating as he is; with little reflection you know that you are not supposed to commit murder and that killing him is part of an expression of anger. You must not hesitate to pay taxes; you will probably be punished if you do not do so. But there are nuances of course. If you decide to ignore cultural regulations—probably after considerable hesitation—you may then have to reflect concerning the method you will use to murder that scoundrel or to avoid taxes (Route 2b). So-called ethical questions, whether pertaining to abortion or homeless people, that confront modern cities demand and receive considerable reflection in the absence of mandatory values.

In most societies one rule is emphasized from an early age: do not be impulsive. For obvious social and moral reasons, children eventually must learn not to urinate and defecate when the urge is upon them but to move or retire to a designated place. According to one competent psychologist, American parents in particular stress the importance of self-control; they discourage restless behavior and " 'wild' running about," so that such behavior declines as children grow older.[5] American teachers in particular encourage reflection not only to curb unruly, disruptive behavior in class but also to improve academic performance in the realms of reading, inductive reasoning, and recall.[6] Ah yes, think before you leap. Perhaps typical of Western attitudes toward hesitancy is a finding that, among American "Caucasian" divorcing parents, those awarded custody of a child or children once tended "to represent themselves in a healthier fashion" and also— on a standardized personality test—to indicate that they could "cope with feelings of anger and impulsivity more effectively," to be "more trusting and open toward others," and to be more sensible regarding alcohol than their former husbands or wives who had not been given custody by the court.[7] To be a responsible parent, therefore, these struggling persons knew it was necessary to claim or to believe that they were not impulsive if they were to retain custody.

Cultural rules mandate or at least encourage patience which means that principals must learn and realize that their status prevents them from achieving certain goals in the immediate future. Children, no matter how strong their impulses, must wait until they have become adults to attain what they then believe to be independence. In a Moroccan village, married women overcome "very low status" in their new households after they have had children; their status is further improved later when as mothers-in-law they possess "formal authority" over their daughters-in-law and influence their own sons.[8] Patience of this sort requires procrastination with sufficient reflection to remind oneself of the cultural regulations and to anticipate changes in status.

Seeking and finding a way to secure release from mandatory cultural rules and duties is likely to be difficult for principals who consequently hesitate some time before plunging into the unknown or the uncharted. Revolutionaries must first convince potential followers that the anticipated new is preferable to the experienced old. In the Communist Manifesto of 1848 the workers of the old world were asked to unite because, they were told, they had nothing to lose but their chains: no one hesitates to be free from chains and hence little or no reflection is needed to achieve a better state by joining the forces of change. We may struggle against the restrictions that engulf us, and yet there may remain a comfortable feeling about the status quo from which there is no immediate or easy escape. Does the old always demand less hesitation than the new?

Cultural Determinism

As observers we might intuitively expect the tendency of principals to lean toward impulsivity or reflection either generally, concerning particular events, or in particular situations to vary from society to society and hence to have a mandatory basis within the rules and duties of each society. Such an expectation stems from the undoubted fact of cultural variability in most spheres of human activity, but provides, however, only preliminary if useful insight into hesitation as a background factor. In the present section emphasis is placed upon the lamentable shortcomings of cultural explanations and the reasons therefor.

It is clear that generalizations concerning an entire society are hazardous because, aside from intuitive guesses, different samples and different modes of measurement have been employed to establish central tendencies within different societies. One brave scholar, after acknowledging these difficulties, presents a chart that seeks to characterize persons in Western countries on the basis of empirical data. Only two traits presumably have implications for hesitation; Austria, for example, is rated high in "neuroticism" with a tendency toward extraversion, and Ireland is low in "neuroticism" with a very slight tendency toward introversion.[9] But one would have to be still braver to claim that Austrians hesitate more or less than the Irish, and yet—well, the temptation to do so is a trifle overpowering.

On occasion a study provides data that run counter in part to intuition concerning cultural determinism. When a direct effort was once made to compare urban and rural Aboriginal and Anglo-Australian children by means of five tests of "cognitive style" perhaps related to hesitation (including the Matching Test) and two standardized tests of nonverbal intelligence, not style so measured but psychometric intelligence accounted for the superiority in reading and mathematics achievement of the non-Aboriginal groups over the Aborigines and of the urban over the rural Aborigines. Psychometric intelligence was measured perforce in a manner favoring non-Aborigines and urban individuals.[10] We do not know whether the Aborigines' original mode of hesitation had been altered by contact with Australian or Western society. Another example: on the Matching Test there was once no difference with respect to accuracy when samples of middle-status Mexican and American children were compared; but the lower-status Mexicans were less accurate and there was also a tendency for both Mexican groups, especially those of lower status, to respond more rapidly than the American children.[11] Why more rapidly? American tourists might imagine that the Mexican children would respond more slowly, for living there seems more leisurely. Does the empirical finding mean that the Mexicans are less patient or less reflective than their neighbors to the north on a test designed in the North? Even if that question were answerable, the presence of individual differences among the Mexicans would intrude. Actually another study of Mexican children by one of the same investigators and with the same test confirmed the view that some of the Mexican children responded quickly but randomly; others collected information until they believed they had found the correct variant; and still others, though also collecting information, eventually gave up in despair and responded randomly.[12] The different approaches of these children to the same test cannot be easily linked to varying conditions in their society or immediate milieu.

If there are differences with respect to hesitation from society to society, the explanation is to be found in their historical development that reflects the environment and past events. Dipping into origins is difficult because, more often than not, the principals themselves are not aware or fully aware of the factors in the past that influence their present judgments. Suppose it were really true, as has been said of Americans, that "we want to assimilate the Jews, but they on the whole refuse with probable justification to be assimilated; the Negroes want to be assimilated, but we refuse to let them assimilate."[13] Then we would have a culturally determined situation that affects and reflects the judgments of Americans of these two groups. No single American, Jew, or black can be said to have originated such a belief, rather it has resulted from social contacts and experiences over the years and then, nevertheless, it influences present hesitation regarding social acceptance. Principals are dependent upon observers—historians, anthropologists, or all those who knowingly or unknowingly transmit traditions to succeeding generations—to locate, even explain origins. And they themselves are not in agreement, as becomes immediately evident when economic factors are weighted by historians with a liberal or a Marxist orientation.

One fact—yes, I think it is a fact—suggests that socialization practices vary not only from society to society,[14] but also within each society; and they are likely to affect principals' modal degrees of hesitation. Do mothers nurse or feed their infants on demand when they cry? How soon must children learn to wait before eating as they grow older? We enter a subtle domain. Consider what at first may seem to be a far-fetched illustration: the birth order of American presidents from George Washington to John F. Kennedy and of British Prime Ministers from Robert Walpole in the eighteenth century to Harold Macmillan in the twentieth century. Those who assumed leadership positions during impor-

tant crises and wars tended—and the word must be *tended*—
to be first-born; those during peaceful times and internal adjustments tended to be middle-born; those during the col-
lapse of social functions and civil conflict tended to be only
children; and those during revolutions tended to be last
born.[15] Other personal and social factors certainly determined the ascension of these men into leadership roles, but
their experience with parents and, if any, siblings may well
have had an effect upon the kinds of situations in their countries with which they convinced their electorate or party
members they could cope; then as leaders they became active or passive leaders. A firstborn, for example, may learn a
leadership style enabling him to be assertive vis-à-vis his
brother or sister which he may use when confronted with
opponents later in life; then some problems and not others
produce varying degrees of hesitation.

On a less speculative level we have evidence both support-
ing and modifying such a birth-order hypothesis. On the one
hand, it was once established that firstborns seemed to be
less depressed, less anxious, and more inclined to have higher
self-esteem than later-born siblings[16]—and therefore were they
less prone to hesitate longer or in situations requiring leadership? On the other hand, it has been convincingly demonstrated, though mostly conventionally, that, although certain abilities or actions are associated with birth order, actual
experience also plays a role; thus first-borns may perform
better than their younger siblings when they are very young,
but they may lose this advantage at age three or four until
their "early teens" when they then regain it "possibly per-
manently."[17]

In addition there are also bits of evidence indicating the
effects of the actual socializers upon subsequent degrees of
hesitation. In one experiment American mothers were observed teaching their second-grade children to remember two
dozen pictures they had seen. The mothers considered reflective as measured by the Matching Test tended to tell their
children to organize the materials into conceptual categories
as they themselves demonstrated this strategy, whereas impulsive mothers only pointed to the pictures. The children

with the reflective mothers subsequently recalled more items than the pitiful tots with the impulsive mothers.[18]

As the evidence on birth order suggests, however, socialization is not the magic key that unlocks all the portals at the entrance to hesitation. While it is true that a long tradition, epitomized by Freud and most sociologists, emphasizes the enduring influence of early experiences within the family or the peer group, it also is probably true that people—at least in the West—may change significantly as a result of adult experiences in their occupations and as they marry and become parents.[19] The impulsive youth turns out to be a responsible mother or father, although her or his reaction to relatively new situations may continue to resemble those acquired in childhood days. Most parents probably know, and many children eventually discover, moreover, that the personalities and other traits of two or more generations are not invariant. Sons are similar to their fathers in some respects, and dissimilar in others. After an investigator once measured selected traits, and a computer and he squeezed the data statistically with sufficient perseverance, he could proclaim that, although somewhat dissimilar, the pairs were also similar in some respects.[20] An impulsive mother, consequently, may be more likely to have an impulsive daughter or son unless the child rebels or has other experiences making her or him inclined to be quite the opposite kind of person.

Yet another blow to socialization as the exclusive factor related to cultural determinism comes from the changes that occur during the lifetime of individuals. When a society changes or when the principals come in contact with a different society, their established modes of judging and acting may be challenged, with the result that hesitation may increase in the absence of their previous rules and duties (Route 1b). In the 1980s a boy who had moved from East to West Berlin, while the city was divided, reported that he had "a big problem" in the bookstores:

In [East Germany] the problem was that everything was Marx and Lenin—very one-sided. But I knew where I stood. Here I can find

anything from books by neo-Nazis to I don't know what. How's a
person supposed to decide what's true? I'm not sure any more *what*
I'm supposed to think.[21]

The lad, according to his testimony, was compelled by the
new situation to reflect; according to him, what he had allegedly learned or been told on the other side of the Wall
had provided less hesitating replies to Critical Questions. In
at least a literary sense both human beings and animals respond similarly to "a change in the complex of stimuli im-
pinging upon them"; their hesitation "elicits more investi-
gating, sniffing, manipulation, and so on."[22]

Finally, just as cultural rules and duties as well as socialization practices usually induce different responses among
principals, so the reaction to events is not uniform. A sociologist, on the basis of interviews collected from a sample of
New Yorkers at the beginning and end of a decade, once noted
"increased rates of cohabitation and illicit drug use" which
he attributed to overall changes in traditional roles within
the society during the 1970s and the 1980s.[23] With relatively
little reflection a particular person may have decided to have
a prolonged or temporary affair with her or his loved one or
to experience drugs without appreciating the consequences.
But not everyone followed the alleged trend; for them the
older rules and duties remained unchanged. Americans whose
marriages "turn bad" and whose "other components of love
fade or turn into the opposite," nevertheless, may have continued to feel some "attachment" to each other: significant
remnants remained, so that these persons did not or could
not hesitate to change appreciably their emotional life or
routines.[24]

In concluding this section, I quite agree that the discussion of the possible effects of cultural and societal factors
upon hesitation has been somewhat disappointing. Yes, general insight is always obtained when the context of hesitation is specified, but the exceptions and the alternative explanations of the details are staggering. The precise degree
of hesitation, in short, is not to be traced to such general
background factors but must be sought in the personalities

of the principals. At the same time the influence of the prevailing culture will not be too drastically underestimated.
Each society resolves certain challenging problems, as a result of which hesitation is diminished. Why is the person sick?
If physicians in modern society believe they know how and
why his illness develops, they or the patients can provide an
explanation with little hesitation; if the relevant knowledge
is missing, they must ponder and reflect. In a society in which
such deterministic knowledge is lacking, there may be greater
hesitation or else a fate-destiny doctrine is impulsively invoked. Above all, it dare not be forgotten that cultural influences may function, as when two persons fall in love, "spontaneously," without conscious realization that the norms of
the society have been ingested.[25]

Language

The tone changes: after hesitating to pay unbounded tribute to cultural determinism as an unhesitating explanation
of hesitation, it is mandatory to express less reservation concerning the role of language. Indeed, language merits close
scrutiny because paradoxically it promotes understanding by
diminishing or increasing hesitation. Either function is closely
related to the principals' culture and society. The linguistic
symbols with which we are provided or which we ourselves
provide usually affect our thoughts, judgments, and the ways
in which we store most of our information and experience.
While it is true, in the profound quip of the poet Paul Valéry,
that "seeing is forgetting the name of the thing one sees"[26]
and hence sensations register with a minimum of hesitation,
the labelling of what is perceived after greater hesitation has
distinct advantages. If you are not a geologist or do not possess his vocabulary, can you describe the kinds of rocks and
stones you find in your environment? In your ignorance do
you hesitate and pause as you try to classify a geological
formation you suddenly or slowly perceive? Some evidence
suggests that performance is improved when previous experience is stored verbally in memory rather than nonver-
bally.[27] Significant values of a society are embodied and

quickly expressed in many of its sentences. Principals in both traditional and Western societies who tend toward "modernity" in the Western sense, for example, are likely to disapprove of the maxim that "it is better to live pretty much for today and let tomorrow take care of itself" and to voice approval for "the traditional ways from the past are not always the best, they need to be changed."[28]

Learning a language is mandatory, for thus principals— whether children or adults—are able to respond to other persons with diminished hesitation, as is quickly discovered when one seeks to decode an unfamiliar foreign language. Illustrations tumble upon us. "The bird crossed the barnyard"; "The hunter shot at the bird overhead"[29]—any English speaker knows with little hesitation that the word "bird" in those two sentences refers to two different animals which, however, share some common attributes. A cultural element is transparent when two persons meet and one says, "How are you?" The question is almost always accepted as a greeting and not as an inquiry concerning the individual's physical or mental health;[30] or, as some wag has suggested, a stranger or a friend is likely to be shocked if you respond in English to the recently fashionable "Have a good day", not with "thanks" or a repetition of the cliché, but with "No, I have other plans."

The mandatory requirement of language is evident in modern societies which stress the importance of punctuality. "Let us meet at two o'clock today": we immediately know that reference is being made to time as measured by clocks in accordance with a system of the particular time zone in which we live. "Let's meet this afternoon"—some hesitation is likely since the time has not been precisely defined. But, on occasion, the precision rule is suspended, and the meaning is grasped without much hesitation. The familiar formula, "once upon a time", that launches many fairy tales[31] is acceptable without an impulse to consult an historical record.

Languages contain mandatory rules that require obedience with little hesitation. These rules pertain not only to grammar—"he is here," not "he are there"—but also to choice of vocabulary. A Swedish scholar had devoted 450 pages to locating forms of address in which the third person is used and the nominative replaces the vocative case. His citations come from Egyptian and other ancient languages, from Chinese, and from languages in developing and European countries. "What does your Majesty wish?" "Would Madam like to take a seat?"[32] In most of these instances it is mandatory for the speaker to abandon the usual "you" without appreciable hesitation in order to be polite or reverential. In European languages there are familiar and formal forms for "you," such as *tu* and *du* for the former and *vous* and *Sie* for the latter in French and German. Some greater hesitation, however, may intrude. The word *Sie* in German means either *you* or *they* when followed by a plural verb; the distinction is not made in the spoken language, but is perfectly clear in the written language since the word there is capitalized when it is used formally in the second person plural; in addition, the identical *sie* also means "she" when it is in lower case (except of course at the beginning of a sentence) and also when its verb is in the third person singular. Almost always, I have noticed, the person being addressed in German comprehends the referent with little or no reflection. A principal, however, may sometimes hesitate: what age must a person reach before it becomes obligatory to use the formal rather than the familiar form when speaking to him? Or, when do two people know each other well enough to abandon the formal *Sie* and substitute the hospitable *du*?

Beyond crude or "basic" communication, forms may be elective rather than mandatory and hence greater hesitation is required.[33] A content analysis of the roughly 400,000 words in a standard American unabridged dictionary has revealed 17,953 terms for human traits: one quarter are judged to be neutral, another quarter to refer to moods and causal or temporary forms of conduct, slightly more than a quarter to evaluation, and the remainder to miscellaneous conditions.[34] Obviously, speakers of the English language potentially have an embarrassment of riches from which to choose in order to enable them to respond impulsively or to reflect concerning the appropriate words to employ.

Although speakers of a particular language may be able to describe any referent, languages differ with respect to the ease or difficulty with which the appropriate word or phrase can be located. In English the word "uncle" obviously can refer to four different relationships: mother's brother or brother-in-law or father's brother or brother-in-law. If you are told that a person is someone's uncle, you are compelled by a cultural limitation of English to hesitate concerning the relationship. In many languages, on the other hand, two or more of these relatives have distinctive terms even as the words "uncle" and "aunt" in English unambiguously reveal at least the person's gender. In those languages, on the other hand, terms for color are less easily codable than corresponding terms in English. In the Ewe language in West Africa, for example, there is a two-syllable word that can be applied to "colors ranging from pitch black to dark grey and including blue."[35] Ewe speakers, however, perceive and can label the difference in these colors by adding descriptive terms, even as English speakers specify the relationship of the person. To ease the linguistic burden and hence to diminish hesitation in common speech, speakers of a language may use words or expressions from another language when the rough equivalent in their own vocabulary has slightly different connotations—try finding a concise, adequate translation of "faux pas" in English.

Not only do English speakers have a rich vocabulary from which to select their modes of expression, and their audiences likewise an equally rich one to which they respond, but there is also a "vast" figurative domain at the disposal of both parties. One list includes "puns, jokes, riddles, stories . . . hyperboles, similes, metaphors, personifications, proverbs, ironic statements, and various other literary tropes."[36] Oh, while consulting a dictionary, add meiosis: after quite a few drinks that rascal smashed some antique furniture and later reported that "he was a little intoxicated."[37]

From among these linguistic riches, metaphors are selected for extensive treatment because they clearly pervade a language. When the concept is defined broadly as "any replacement of one word by another, or any identification of one thing, concept, or person with any other," it has been shown that every grammatical part of speech from nouns to prepositions has undergone such substitution in the poetry of fifteen British poets extending from Chaucer to Dylan Thomas (including T. S. Eliot).[38] If a metaphor makes "the strange familiar and the familiar strange"[39] and if it is "a solar eclipse [that] hides the object of study and at the same time reveals some of its most salient and interesting characteristics when viewed through the right telescope,"[40] using and responding to such a verbal device may require degrees of hesitation greater than conventional language.

Most writers on metaphors, however, distinguish between dead or foreign and live or novel metaphors.[41] The origins of the dead ones may be found in learned historical treatises concerning the development of a language in a society, but may be and probably are ignored or are unknown to most principals who use them. In English, for example, we can refer to "the foot of the mountain" without thinking of human anatomy, or we call a person "strait-laced" without ever knowing or recalling an undergarment.[42] In contrast, were I to label a sentence "elephantine" or a person "buttoned up," I would be possibly inventing a metaphor which, after hesitating and groaning, you might generously call a live one. Dead metaphors require a little hesitation when once they have been learned and when their use as figures of speech is not questioned.

Live and especially novel metaphors, on the other hand, may demand reflection before they can be selected or understood. There are exceptions of course: some live metaphors, perhaps brilliantly original ones, can be coined and comprehended in a poetic flash with little or no hesitation. Once, when the principals were asked to complete incomplete sentences, college students and preschoolers "proved more lively" and "imaginative" than elementary school children in producing endings such as "sad as a pimple," "weather as boiling as your head popping open." The preschoolers may have been making a "virtue out of necessity": with their meager vocabulary they felt impelled to "overextend" words and they emerged with "a middle-aged piece of cake" and, for tight shoes, "my toes are huddled together."[43]

Upon reflection I think we must agree that the abstract quality of metaphors is not different from most everyday concepts. The word "dog" is used to refer to a large variety of animals which differ in size, shape, color, configuration but which share a biological attribute; and "dogged" applied to a person as a metaphorical adjective also refers to a variety of evaluated behavior. Words of this sort acquire very specific meanings and connotations. Can John Smith "fly"? We do not define flying merely in terms of the ability to lift oneself off the ground. When John jumps "five centimeters," we do not call that feat flying: it may satisfy our loose definition of flying but conventionally it is "not what we call flying."[44] The context of the convention is also unhesitatingly relevant, for does not John "fly" when he boards an airplane to travel from one city to another? You should not call these examples trivial as you contemplate them in relation to common abstractions such as "democracy," "beauty," and "individuality," words loaded with affect and having significant social and political implications.

When the users of words hesitate concerning their meaning and when pointing is impossible or impractical, different methods of defining them have been found to be available, such as contextual location ("eye?" "part of the body"); range of inclusion ("art?" "a painting, music, dance, etc."); feelings and emotions ("monster?" "it frightens people and [they] probably enjoy it"); function or role ("bottle?" "you can drink from it"); the judgments, opinion, and values it arouses ("law?" "most of it is bad or unjust; and the rest is superfluous"); and sixteen other devices.[45] And then there are dictionaries that provide definitions of individual words like "oxymoron" and, if kept up to date, "wimp".

The words and expressions so far considered are obviously embodied in a context, beginning with a sentence and a paragraph and ending sometimes with a series of volumes. The combinations, we know, are infinite. Why is language so versatile? The answer must point to the enormous number of external and internal events to which reference must be made if information, impressions, and judgments are to be stored, expressed, and comprehended. Consider quickly the discoveries of science or the creative insights of sensitive poetry. Some language here is mandatory, but much more is elective. Principals who are unable to label their feelings may therefore feel uncomfortable without appreciating the reasons for their emotional state. Someone who is unemployed or who no longer works because he has reached the age of compulsory retirement will be able to provide a number of explanations for his discomfort. A young person will say, perhaps, that he and his family need the money he used to earn; the older person may suggest that he "misses" what he used to do five days a week or that being retired means he has come closer to death. What would either person say were he told that the following are "deep-seated needs in most people who strive to make some sense out of their existence?"

They need to structure their day; they need wider social experiences; they need to partake in collective purposes (and they want the products that result from collective action); they need to know where they stand in society in comparison with others in order to clarify their personal identity; and they need regular activities.[46]

The unemployed or the retired person may immediately recognize that his present status does not enable him to satisfy these "needs" sufficiently or at all and therefore contributes to his malcontent. Providing him with labels corresponding to the above list would enable him more clearly, with greater precision or with less hesitation to comprehend his condition. In fact, when once any kind of behavior is labelled—you are eating too much; that is illegal—the principal is likely to be affected and thereafter to react impulsively or, after reflecting, to respond appropriately according to his own view of both the label and the situation.[47] Labelling of this sort can stigmatize phenomena ranging from deviance in the view of a psychiatrist or a policeman to the sight of luscious food as it appears to a gourmet or a person trying to limit his caloric intake. Language, by thus reducing hesitation and increasing impulsive judgments, enables principals carefully or carelessly to express generalizations that may in fact be true or false. A brilliant psychologist once used a relevant simile when he wrote that "concepts and words are like sponges," and he added that "while it is not easy to dry a wet sponge entirely and quickly, it sometimes seems almost impossible to remove from a concept those value-qualities which it has once absorbed."[48] Whether characterizing literature, turmoil, the weather, or a holiday, most historians, journalists, and the rest of us may not hesitate when reference is made to a century (romanticism), a decade (the sixties), a year (of the drought), or even a week or day (vacation, Christmas); the time period thus becomes tagged and, when mentioned again and again, it may give the impression that it has not been artificially or arbitrarily postulated by human beings but is as natural as sunrise and sunset.

Since language must be learned by children as they are socialized, it is to be anticipated that American psychologists have devised paper-and-pencil schedules to determine how principals comprehend various figures of speech.[49] In one of them the subject is given eighteen incomplete sentences, one at a time, and is asked to select in each case one of four endings that are provided; thus, "The weather was as warm as . . . " is followed by "the warmest day in spring," "toast in the early morning," "the smile of a friend you haven't seen for years," and "a shoestring lying in the middle of the floor."[50] In another, three chromatic pictures are displayed (for example: an old man, a gnarled tree, and a wooden rocking chair) and the principal is asked to select the two that "go together" best and to explain the reason for the pairing.[51] Investigations of this type tentatively suggest, for American principals, a relation between the ability to comprehend and to produce various figures of speech, including metaphors.[52] For young children verbal learning is reported to be slow: as they are instructed verbally concerning permitted and tabooed activities, perhaps they must be given an explicit ("do only this, but not that") rather than an implicit ("do only this") communication,[53] so that comprehension becomes less impulsive and is not affected by a momentary goal. In a changing society adults must likewise learn new linguistic expressions. "That decision of the Oval Office:" if you are an American, you instantly and impulsively identify those who made the decision, but do you also know that the rhetorical device of synecdoche is being illustrated? Similes, on the other hand, herald the presence of a verbal device with "like" or "as" and hence may require a moment of reflection. Metaphors and the other figures may also be misunderstood and require varying degrees of hesitation before being decoded. Within each specialized group, whether it be dominated by scholars, publishers, elitists, criminals, or ethnic peers, somewhat distinctive jargon and sentence structure are mandatory and comprehended. Such jargon and modes of expression may be misunderstood by members of out-groups. Compromises may be necessary for the sake of intelligibility. The heart, for example, may be referred to as a pump, and light as a wave because non-physiologists and non-physicists who think they know something about pumps and waves can more easily and with less hesitation comprehend an aspect of the phenomena.[54]

Language is only one of the ways in which principals communicate with one another. A publication called *Journal of Nonverbal Behavior* has been appearing since 1976, which is a tribute to the ingenuity displayed by investigators of this communication form. One article, for example, reviews six different theories that would seek "to account for the dyadic exchange of messages that communicate intimacy, immediacy, or involvement" without the use of language; thus "deviation from expectancy" is the action conveying intimacy.[55] Writing requires more hesitation than verbal expression before it can be inscribed since the principal is likely to know that his words and sentences will probably be subject to greater scrutiny; whether spoken or recorded words and sentences can be more readily comprehended probably depends upon the principal's own experience and inclination; the latter, however, can be reexamined when necessary or desired. In one analysis fifty-four societies are divided into those in which the system of writing has been alphabetic or phonetic and those in which it has been mnemonic or entirely absent. Associated with the former or more complicated system of writing rather than with the latter is a tendency to be characterized by agriculturally intensive food production, larger towns or cities, greater full-time occupational specialization, the use of money in economic exchange, and the presence of full-time religious officials.[56] No causal connection between these tendencies is assumed, and yet the need to reflect because of the writing system may have been associated with societies possessing the complex cultures. On the other hand, it can be argued that those societies without writing must also preserve their traditions and, as it were, their records; and past events have been transmitted by specified persons such as praise singers who use oral media.[57] Their audiences may have to hesitate initially before learning the traditional, historical facts and the rules of the society; but thereafter recognition and recall function with a minimum of hesitation.

Certainly persons who are "functionally illiterate" in a Western society—"unable to read and write well enough to meet the basic requirements of everyday life"—usually must hesitate longer than those who are literate. Those with the handicap in the West cannot immediately select the packaged foods they seek in a supermarket unless the labels offer pictures of the contents; they cannot guide themselves by street signs in strange neighborhoods; they cannot identify the bus they would take by glancing at the sign signifying its route or destination. What the roughly estimated twenty-three to twenty-seven million illiterates in the United States must do is obtain such information after hesitating: they must carefully search for cues that will help them or they must invent some excuse to save themselves embarrassment by seeking help from bystanders.[58]

IN SHORT: not unexpectedly, although the rules of a society and its culture as well as the ensuing duties affect the values of their populations, they provide only preliminary if significant insight into the fluctuating degrees of hesitancies generally but not exclusively prevalent therein; indeed, the language people speak and to which they respond offer specifically valuable, perhaps too numerous clues to their impulsivity and reflection.

4

Personality

Throughout the previous discussion of culture and society it has been impossible not to hesitate to puncture generalizations by suggesting possible exceptions. Under certain circumstances some principals rather than others tend to be impulsive or reflective, even though their culture is similar and they live in the same society. What are those circumstances? At any moment the principal's judgment or action, or both, depend upon the nature of the situation at hand, persons who are also present or assumed to be relevant to the situation, and the personality of the principal himself. Although these variables of situations, persons, and personality interact, a separate chapter will be devoted to each with frequent references to their interaction. We begin with personality.

Rarely is a principal concerned directly with the hesitation required to judge or to act. Instead he deals effectively or ineffectively with problems and events, as a psychologist has proclaimed, through "visual exploration, grasping, crawling and walking, attention and perception, language and thinking, exploring novel objects and places, manipulating the surroundings, and producing effective changes in environment."[1] Hesitation is a byproduct as we tangle with the Critical Questions: What will we do, can we do it, may or must we do it, what will the consequences be, and so on? Or it is assessed in retrospect: why did it take me so long to make up my mind?

Degrees

Within a societal or cultural context degrees of hesitation are to be attributed to locatable aspects of the personality. At first glance an exception to that statement would seem to be the so-called "startle pattern," a rapid sequence of muscular movements beginning at the head and extending downward over the body in response to sudden, intensive, acoustic stimulation. Experiments with animals and human beings reveal that, even though the reaction occurs within a fraction of a second, its latency and amplitude may be affected by prior stimulation too weak by itself to produce the startle, by the actual intensity of the stimulation, and by drugs; and its amplitude may be augmented by another prior stimulus such as a light that has been conditioned to arouse fear or anxiety. These effects probably result not from an overloading of the nervous system but from the activation of specific, higher neural centers.[2] Thus a basic or primitive startle pattern can be affected by the individual's prior sensory experience, even though the experience has been very brief.

In contrast, consider a principal who "involuntarily" stutters. Presumably stuttering is not fostered in any society and is never highly valued, at least on a conscious level, by stutterers themselves, who unwittingly interrupt their own speech, and are unable to pronounce a particular word or complete a sentence before hesitating some length of time. In spite of a strong desire to continue speaking or to reply to a question quickly and normally, the individual who has been fluently expressing his thoughts suddenly begins to hesitate and may feel embarrassed or self-conscious: try as he would, something within him causes his lips to tremble and, as he keeps repeating the same syllable, he is distressed. That something he knows comes from within himself, but it is an annoying part of *me* at odds with the self. Ordinarily such hesitation is considered a handicap; a moral judgment in effect is made when it is called a "disturbance," whether or not the explanation is thought to be related to anxiety.[3] The self of the stutterer resents something within himself, some uncontrollable *me*. One study, however, that compared a very small number of aphasic and normal principals once indicated, of course, that the "pause durations" of the former tended to be longer than those of the latter. Of interest here is the explanations provided for the interruptions: sometimes the principals needed to catch their breath but at other times they must have been reflecting inasmuch as they could not find the precise word or they had difficulty locating the "syntactic sequencing of individual elements in the process."[4]

Among non-stutterers the self rather than the *me* may increase hesitation as the principal also interrupts himself not to pronounce the next syllable but to seek the correct or appropriate word, phrase, or idea.[5] Perhaps inexperience in the past requires reflection in the present; whereas fluency or glibness results from past experience relevant to the current situation (Route 3a). Principals and observers, the variable linkage suggests, may interpret the fluency of speech differently. You telephone a friend and speak at what you believe to be your normal speed, whether or not the telephone is located in your home or in a public place that is only partially enclosed. Although you and an eavesdropper may agree that you are talking with little hesitation, an observer who secretly records the chitchat might discover that your speed is greater in your home than in the public place where you are slightly inhibited by the vague possibility that your precious words may be heard by passersby. Also the reflection required to link any event to the self probably increases the degree of hesitation. If a principal's skin is lacerated, the pain in itself is distasteful, but then additional responses are evoked when the experience is referred to the self: What caused the accident, could it have been fate-destiny? If the pain has been

inflicted by someone else, the person may consider the blow
an insult or an indication that he cannot protect himself; or,
if he believes that only he is responsible, he will blame himself and thereafter lose self-confidence.

Almost always, but not always, the degree of hesitation at
the moment can be traced to the principal's past experience
or background factors: has or has he not hesitated in the
past (Routes 2 and 3 vs. 0)? Human motives or drives give
rise to judgments and actions, but then, except for very basic
biological tendencies such as breathing and voiding, experience functions as a guide to their satisfaction or reduction.
We all must eat, but the precise food we prefer or abhor results from previous gustatory experiences which probably
have cultural components. The principal usually does not have
to hesitate for long: He knows where and when he will be
fed or feed himself; he has definite tastes concerning the foods
he would eat; and as a hunter or a tiny tot he is able to find
the food. These variables affect his verbalized or unverbalized replies to the Critical Questions: what he will, can, may,
must do as well as the consequences, imperatives, intentions, and actual behavior.

The principal himself may not be completely aware, or
perhaps even aware at all, of the past experiences that require or enable him to pass judgments or react with little
hesitation. The so-called Freudian slip by definition is not
premeditated: the speaker spontaneously says something nasty
as a result of hostility he has previously interiorized when
he wishes to be laudatory or polite. Early in this century a
psychologist summarized scholarly observations concerning
perseveration: "Quite against our will, ideas and thoughts in
which we have been deeply interested for some time—melo-
dies, chess games, and the like—may keep coming back into
our minds."[6] He also called attention to hallucinations that
may occur more or less spontaneously.

In other domains the relevant past experience that reduces
hesitation is elusive. The principal, regardless of his sophis-
tication, usually can quickly indicate the painting or photograph he likes; his preference is likely to be the culmination
of past experiences that have affected not only his expressed

or unexpressed aesthetic philosophy but also his moral conceptions of the good or the beneficial life.[7] Consider "spontaneous" laughter or chuckles. According to an old Arme-
nian fable, a man explains why he always plays his cello
with his finger in one place on the same string: "Of course
others move their fingers about constantly. They are looking
for the place. I have found it."[8] To call this funny, principals
must know how cellos are played, and, perhaps, they must
imagine how cellists look when they perform. Only then can
they impulsively respond; prior familiarity with both the instruments and with cellists is essential. We know that, if a
joke has to be explained, and hence requires some reflection,
it loses its punch and may cease to be funny. Similarly a
successful cartoon conveys its creator's message almost instantly and therefore requires the audience to understand the
message with little or no reflection. Be it noted, however,
that personality factors related to hesitation may play a role.
Boys between the ages of six and eight once seemed better
able to comprehend the cartoons they were shown when
classified as reflective rather than either impulsive or slow-
and-inaccurate on the Matching Test, but the latter smiled
and laughed more at what they saw; by the age of ten the
difference in comprehension disappeared; in general, those
classified as fast-accurate could comprehend the cartoons
without affective responses, they seemed "withdrawn and
detached."[9] The audience for a cartoon with a political message looks at the cartoon with considerable preparation; they
know, for example, the physical appearance of the individual being praised or criticized so well that they can instantly
recognize the caricature from a few facial and bodily clues.
Some hesitation, nevertheless, may be required to grasp the
message or to respond to the humor or criticism being portrayed. Even in such a restricted group as American college
students, men and women once claimed that they reacted
differently to the appearance of profanity in cartoons.[10] Un-
surprising, therefore, is the following conclusion based almost exclusively on British principals that "the type of humor preferred by people has tended to correspond with their
personality, interests, and prevailing mood."[11]

Little hesitation occurs in other domains when past experience, though recognized, is not consciously present as judgment is passed. A photograph of another person who is known to the principal or who has recently been seen by him is recognized almost instantly; hesitation is longer when there has been no contact with the other person for years and the photograph realistically displays the changes aging has wrought: That must be the person I once knew, you think. The same kind of hesitating judgment takes place when an actual acquaintance is encountered: you know him instantly or, if time has passed, you more slowly recognize him. But suppose the lad has grown a beard in the interim?

The basis for past and even present hesitation may be more remote. At any given moment the principal realizes whether an organism with visible eyes, animal or human, is looking at him; and it is important to note—*mirabile dictu*—according to available, but quite tentative evidence that "observers label certain facial expressions in the same way regardless of culture . . . unless culture-specific display rules interfere."[12] According to a Hungarian physician, "we can know more than we can tell—we recognize the moods of the human face, without being able to tell, except quite vaguely, by what signs we know it."[13] Although my judgment about your facial expression is probably correct, as you yourself will testify, if I ask you, it is also possible that both of our judgments may be affected by other factors—as has been demonstrated, conventionally[14]—such as our general orientation or our anticipations that we shall be compelled to pass judgment. In addition, it has been shown once that this ability to recognize facial expression may develop gradually as children grow older.[15]

The physician just cited also suggests that any constellation of related pieces can be perceived as a whole, as a Gestalt, with little hesitation or reflection; thus we can quickly comprehend the tenor of oral communication by combining the quality of the voice, the words, the sentences, the style, and the literary composition, each of which can be of interest, yet at the instant of comprehension need not be analyzed in its own right.[16] Halt: a sensible reservation is necessary: "to see a problem is to see something that is hidden," *but* the total perception is "the outcome of an active shaping of experience performed in the pursuit of knowledge." Possibly facial expressions are more important than verbal expressions and bodily movement to convey information about the affective states of others,[17] and therefore in any case the act of looking and interpreting somewhat impulsively what is perceived springs from unverbalized experience.

Upon reflection past experience may be organized in order to facilitate both learning and memory and hence to reduce hesitation in the future (Route 3a). What has been called "chunking" occurs even on a simple level: stimulus information is regrouped or recoded so that it can be more easily stored.[18] The seven digits comprising American, Canadian, and other telephone numbers are grouped into an introductory set of three followed by the remaining four; and more recently the last four and even all seven have been expressed by commercially motivated and other organizations in meaningful words whose letters correspond to positions on telephone dials. As a consequence of such organization the routes to be followed are usually recognized, immediately, with little hesitation when their ever-present, almost compulsory atttributes are noted. Like it or not, we are creatures of habit, we know or imagine we know what we must do to achieve a goal (Potentiality), little or no reflection at the moment is required. We believe we have a plan of action, a more or less conscious "script."[19] With such equipment there need be little hesitation, a course of action is available, and the destination or goal is known or assumed to be reasonable. Often, though not always, the principal realizes what he must do in order to achieve a particular goal and, when the occasion arises, he does just that with little or no reflection, even as the hungry infant responds to the available breast or bottle when he is hungry, as the young girl finds her way home when she is not going off on an adventure with her peers, or as adults know the tasks they are expected to perform at work under normal circumstances.

Familiarity may decrease hesitation, but the event or the

situation must be specified. Canadian students once were able to find spelling errors more quickly and more accurately in familiar than in unfamiliar prose passages.[20] They had been deliberately told, however, to find the errors; if they had not been alerted and instead had been reading normally, they might not have noticed the errors even in the familiar words, or they might have noticed fewer errors because under normal circumstances they would have been impulsively attempting to comprehend the meaning of the word. Familiarity can breed carelessness as any proofreader discovers to his sorrow. And then impulsive perception may also stimulate reflection when the principal is suitably motivated (Route 2b). You look at a drawing or a painting but only later do you begin to appreciate either the artist's intention or its subtleties. Whether they are disciples of Freud or a mystic sect, principals almost never can interpret their own dreams immediately upon awakening. The origin and the possible symbols can be appreciated only through hesitant contemplation or, in the case of psychoanalysis, with the aid of a competently or incompetently trained professional.

A principal may witness an event that he has never exactly experienced before: someone calls for help in a burning building or in a rough sea, and he is the only person nearby who can effect the rescue. But what does he do in this new and perplexing situation? We believe we know that innumerable background factors from his past—such as his relationship to that individual, the uniqueness of the situation, and his own moral philosophy concerning atruism[21]—affect him as he quickly reaches a decision, so that little actual habituation or hesitation may be apparent as a judgment is reached and an action or no action follows.

So-called Traits

Inasmuch as the degree of hesitation varies with the relation of the judgment and behavior to the self as well as with the principal's past experiences, it becomes necessary to inquire whether the individual is or can be considered consistent with respect to the extent to which he hesitates in a variety of situations. We thus face full square the problem of traits concerning which psychologists and all the rest of us are in disagreement: is it either necessary or useful to postulate a general tendency to judge or behave consistently in a variety of situations during either a restricted or extended period of time? This problem of consistency in the present or the future is not confined to hesitation, and arises in connection with most judgments and behavior. More generally, we know both intuitively and empirically that every principal is consistent to some extent but may be inconsistent with reference to some persons or in some situations. Do you always tell the truth and therefore consider honesty one of your traits, can you not visualize circumstances in which a white lie enables you to achieve your goal or is morally desirable? Here is an issue that cannot be settled once and for all and therefore the word "trait" hereafter will be enclosed in quotation marks in order to remind us of the problem's baffling status.

Let us begin with perhaps the most prolonged analysis of impulsivity as measured by various paper-and-pencil questionnaires designed by British psychologists and their colleagues.[22] I tremble to try to summarize their voluminous publications because they are likely to have released another study before this paragraph or even this sentence has been completed. They assume that "personality" can best be understood in terms of "traits" or dispositions that are expressed in many but not all situations. One of these "traits" they call "impulsiveness" which, as previously indicated during the discussion of Questioning in chapter 2 and on the basis of a factor analysis derived from hundreds of young British adults (including twins and both genders), they think is composed of the four factors labelled narrow impulsiveness, risk-taking, non-planning, and liveliness. Although the four factors have been related to one another and to sociability, and although they have correlated "quite well" with extraversion and psychoticism, these relations have been "not very high", and consequently the authors conclude that "to talk about impulsivity as a general factor is decidedly dangerous."[23]

According to the editor of a book concerned with the "biological bases" of impulsivity and related objects, the "implicit assumption in all approaches is that the traits called extraversion, sensation seeking, and impulsivity share some common phenomenal manifestations, some biological correlates, and, perhaps, some common biological determinism."[24] If such a biological assumption for impulsivity were valid, it might be reasonable to assume the existence of a "trait." Only modest success, however, can be claimed in relating impulsivity to cortical activity as measured by the electroencephalogram; impulsivity in this experiment was determined by having British undergraduates open and close their eyes in response to an experimenter's instructions.[25] The problem has also been attacked directly by studying twins. Various activities of American female twins, with a mean age of ninety-seven months, were once measured and observed. Included was what might be called an indication of their impulsiveness, namely, the time it took them to choose between a visible and hidden toy and a toy with which they were told they could play not immediately but a bit later. They as well as their mothers were questioned concerning their behavior generally. Whether or not the mothers realized that from a scientific viewpoint the twins were or were not identical and hence may have accorded them somewhat similar or dissimilar treatment, there was a tendency in these empirical situations for the identical twins to resemble each other more than the fraternal twins. It is possible, consequently, that "several aspects" of the activity having implications for hesitation have "moderate heritability."[26] Hesitation in this instance thus almost qualifies as a "trait." One of the colleagues of the British psychologists mentioned above, after studying identical twins, has concluded that "about 60 percent of the total reliable variation" not only for impulsivity but also for two other traits (sociability and extraversion) may be "due to hereditary causes."[27] That conclusion is immediately challenged by another researcher on the grounds that genetic and environmental effects can be separated only when identical twins have not been raised in the same environment, that identical twins tend to be treated similarly, and that percentages derived from the interaction of the two effects are misleading.[28] Investigators in the same British laboratory, after examining their own non-twin data, later conclude that "it becomes doubtful when we can talk about impulsivity as a single unitary concept" and they wonder "whether anything survives of 'impulsivity' " after its relation to the other three dispositions (again: risk-taking, non-planning, and liveliness) are "summed."[29] Overall, in short, it looks as if impulsivity as a "trait" has not been impressively tapped by these methods; more evidence is needed, and such evidence is difficult to come by and is not unequivocal.

The search for a "trait" in the United States—but with some replications in two Guatemalean communities and in Israel—has been conducted largely through the use of the Matching Test among children and has been spearheaded by its originator and his collaborators. Children thus classified as reflective, in comparison with those categorized as impulsive, have tended to respond more slowly and more accurately to different, though similar variants of that test;[30] to recall more of what they have read[31] and to make fewer errors in reading; to discover more incongruous elements in pictures; and to reason more slowly and more accurately.[32] The investigators then subscribe to the view that the "major cause of a reflective attitude is anxiety over making a mistake. . . . The reflective [American] child wishes to be correct and therefore tries to avoid mistakes at any cost [and] to avoid the humiliation of being wrong."[33] From evidence of this sort it is thought reasonable to postulate "a generalized behavior tendency to be impulsive (or reflective) in problem situations where the child should consider the validity of the answers"; there must be, in short, a "trait" facilitating such consistency.[34]

That conclusion has been so variously attacked that the originator of the Matching Test has felt impelled to repeat "science's oldest homily: all knowledge is tentative."[35] These criticisms can be briefly reviewed. In the first place, the Matching Test itself, as already indicated when it was described in chapter 2, has been criticized, especially its method of combining latency and error scores. The hesitancy of American kindergarten children, as measured by that test, once tended to be consistent only with respect to additional tests that also involved uncertainty. So-called impulsive and reflective subjects did not differ from one another on items producing "minimal uncertainty,"[36] such as repeating a series of digits produced by an adult.[37] In one experiment, Grade 2 Israeli children were dichotomized by means of the same test, shown thirty-six pictures of common objects and told to find the one picture which the adult had in mind by asking a series of questions. The reflective children asked more general questions ("Is it a toy?") rather than more specific ones ("Is it a doll?") than did the impulsive children, but the efficiency as judged by the number of questions they asked turned out to be similar for both groups. Then, as indicated later in this chapter, children may become more reflective as they grow older, which must mean that the "trait" is not consistent over time. Most important of all, in the Matching Test and similar tests children have been confronted with alternatives from which they must select the correct one. Their tendency to react impulsively or to reflect, consequently, is constrained by the investigator's choice of alternatives. The situation here is realistic since often we must select a course of action predetermined by someone else, yet there are innumerable other situations in which the principal and not an investigator or force external to himself supplies the alternatives. You have a problem to solve, and you and you alone must imagine various solutions before you select one. Or sometimes the alternatives are either to act or not to act: should you adhere to the faith and practices of your forefathers? This matching literature, as already argued in chapter 2, examines a restricted sphere of hesitation and hence the "trait" is confined to restricted judgments and actions probably also within a restricted time period.

Another approach to the "trait" problem is simply to assume a priori that some dimension of hesitation is a central disposition within principals. An influential study before World War II sought to examine the uniqueness of fifty American males of college age by scaling, interviewing, and observing them in forty-four respects. One of these variables was called "impulsion," defined as the "tendency to respond . . . quickly and without reflection" and to be characterized by rapid reaction times, "emotional driveness," absence of foresight, and a tendency to act without a careful plan. The contrasting tendencies were summarized as "deliberation," measured by such items as "I think much and speak little" and "I am slow to fall in love." A sufficiently significant, but somewhat unimpressive relation was found, for example, between this variable and the ability to learn solutions to relatively simple problems such as associating verbal stimuli with pressing a particular telegraph key.[38] Later the entire inventory of forty-four variables was operationalized in greater detail and given to "over a thousand" American male and a like number of American female students. The impulsivity score tended to be negatively related to being precise and definite and to being well-ordered and disciplined; positively related to being playful and pleasure-seeking and to being fickle and unpredictable; and not related at all to being self-protective and defensive and to being well-behaved or seeking recognition.[39] The positive relationships suggest that the "trait" operates only in a restricted sphere.

This effort to assess principals by means of a large battery of tests and observations has led to two impressive enterprises. The first, whose director was the psychologist who had originated the approach in the 1930s, was a unit with eight stations in the United States, Ceylon, China, and India that assessed candidates for the U. S. Office of Strategic Services during World War II in order to determine their assets and liabilities for a variety of positions and responsibilities ranging from analyzing "intelligence" information in Washington to functioning as agents or spies behind enemy lines.[40] The great variety of abilities observed by the staff did not include variables related to hesitation, although some of the assessments probably made references to it. Hesitation, whether a "trait" or not, therefore, was not thought to be relevant to the very practical problem at hand.

The other enterprise was a unit of the American Telephone and Telegraph Company, whose aim was to improve the selection and advancement of managers and to assess their careers as well as their personalities over a period of twenty years. In this project one of the variables was "impulsivity," this time measured by a small battery of existing, standardized personality schedules and, in some instances, through an interview. With one exception, no surprises emerged from the analyses; for example, the well-adjusted individuals tended to have low impulsivity scores. The exception suggests a tendency for those "promoted higher" in the company to be not less but more impulsive, possibly because these persons also were more concerned with "self-development" and were less "security-oriented."[41] The fact that there was little or no relation, especially for the college population, between impulsivity at the outset and twenty years later could indicate that this tendency did not remain stable over time, or, more likely, that the measures being employed lacked sufficient reliability and validity.

These omnibus studies, it may be concluded, have not enthroned impulsivity as a "trait" but, except for the OSS assessment unit, have demonstrated its utility as a practical, common sense measure.

Impulsivity as a general disposition has been similarly included as one of the four dimensions in a study of temperament, defined not in terms of content, but "generally" to include only "the stylistic aspects of behavior." Impulsivity was once operationalized in a questionnaire both for parents as observers of their children as well as for principals, chiefly American students. Parents were asked to rate such items as "Child gets bored easily," "Child goes from toy to toy quickly." The other three dimensions—activity, emotionality, and sociability—were said to qualify as components of temperament, but on the basis of research largely on twins the conclusion was drawn that "a case has not yet been made for impulsivity as a temperament." That case, however, cannot be eternally abandoned, inasmuch as the authors themselves indicate that among American women hysteria may be a combination of "high" impulsivity and "high" emotionality: "Such a person tends to be childish, complaining, impetu-

ous, seductive, and possessed of numerous bodily complaints."[42]

And dreams, do they provide a clue to this "trait" problem
since they might be expected to indicate a deep-seated or
unconscious preference leaning toward impulsivity or reflection? Dream studies, however, concentrate on the contents
and affective tones and provide little reliable information
concerning hesitation. One category in an extremely careful
analysis of dreams reported by American undergraduates is
that of familiarity-unfamiliarity: the setting of the dream;
the characters therein; and the portrayal of friendliness,
misfortune, aggression. There was a very slight but significant tendency for the females to report a higher proportion
of familiar than unfamiliar themes; and for the males another very slight tendency appeared for some but not all of
the familiarity categories in the opposite direction.[43] Now
suppose there is less hesitation in connection with the familiar than the unfamiliar and suppose further that females in
American society are possibly less likely than males to be
exposed to unfamiliar setting. Then, if the results of this study
were more clear-cut, we might have evidence suggesting a
fairly basic tendency for American females to tend to hesitate less than males. Yes, the opposite interpretation is possible with respect to female differences. In either case, however, nothing conclusive emerges from the study that can
justify postulating a hesitancy "trait."

It must be obvious by now that the research directly or
indirectly suggesting or implying that hesitation is a "trait"
remains tantalizing and inconclusive. Actually, hesitation
regarding hesitation is repeated when traits in general, any
traits, are discussed; adherents for and against postulating
such dispositions rather than situational tendencies are conspicuous.[44] We might imagine, for example, that principals
tend to have strong or weak confidence in the validity of their
own beliefs; yet a competent review of studies on this question concludes that attitude strength is "not a master dimension."[45] It is likewise precarious to assume that even a truly
dramatic or traumatic experience may be generalized, and

hence have implications for hesitation. Jewish survivors of the Holocaust were once compared with Israeli Jews of the same age who had not been in Nazi concentration camps and who consequently were not expected to have feelings of guilt associated with their own survival. The two groups did not differ with respect to feelings of guilt they might have had in situations in which they had been ignoble, self-destructive (overdrinking alcoholic beverages), behaving contrary to a moral code, or disruptive with respect to social relations. No semblance of a "trait" here.[46]

Interrelations

With sufficient statistical or experimental ingenuity and originality, investigators have been able to relate hesitation to a longish list of human tendencies or behavior that frequently includes dispositions such as anxiety, intelligence, and sociability and sometimes even physiological reactions.[47] In almost all instances the relations are moderate or low, though statistically significant. These findings are not the least bit surprising or enlightening since different methods of measuring hesitation and the other tendencies have been employed and since, after all, a temporal or accuracy element is involved in all human activity. You certainly may select almost any tendency you wish and eventually show that it is related to impulsivity or reflection. In each study tentative knowledge is acquired which may be a bit more helpful than common sense and in some instances provides a tentative solution to a momentarily perlexing question. Once the hesitation of American boys was measured by means of the Matching Test and they were also asked to indicate the alternative they would be likely to select when confronted with an everyday petty problem, such as what they would do if someone pushed ahead of them in a line of boys waiting to drink water at a fountain. Would the reflective or the impulsive boys choose to be direct and hence assertive or to be aggressive more frequently than impulsive ones, and which of the two groups would decide to be passive and complain to some authority? The questions might be answered either way; in actual fact, the reflective boys tended to select the direct approach of confronting the intruder, the impulsive ones the passive approach.[48] In many experimental situations, moreover, we have no way of knowing whether or not hesitation has played a role. American preschoolers were once more favorably impressed by characters whose happiness or sadness resulted from having performed a socially acceptable rather than an unacceptable action;[49] we can only surmise that the children must have reflected somewhat before they could pass judgment concerning the happiness of the characters and the acceptability of their causes.

When we tentatively or semi-permanently abandon hesitation as a trait, we cannot avoid observing that some principals hesitate more or less than others in a variety of situations. They may not reveal the consistency demanded before a trait can be postulated: but they do have dispositions, if not necessarily consistent ones, to be impulsive or to reflect. Such dispositions are likely to function in conjunction with other tendencies requiring varying degrees of hesitation and thus to provide essential background information. In the following list of candidates the selection is admittedly arbitrary, though carefully made, and the relevance to hesitation is cautiously suggested:

1. *Sensation-seeking.* Analysis of data obtained from English and American students revealed four components of this scale that have been baptized thrill and adventure seeking, experience seeking, disinhibition, and boredom susceptibility. Those components once correlated significantly if not dramatically with scores indicating extraversion, absence of fear in situations involving the possibility of physical harm, favorable attitudes toward risky behavior and gambling, tolerance of intense stimuli, and dozens of other traits.[50] Perhaps favorable tendencies in those respects indicate some inclination to respond impulsively.

2. *Open vs. closed mind.* Fruitful research, based largely on various paper-and-pencil questionnaires but including behavioral measures under laboratory conditions, has explored "the extent to which the person can receive, evaluate, and act on relevant information received from the outside on its

own intrinsic merits, unencumbered by irrelevant factors in the situation arising from within the person or from the outside."[51] Perhaps a principal with a closed mind finds it unnecessary to reflect and tends to respond impulsively; one with an open mind reflects as he receives and evaluates new information.

3. *Purpose in Life.* Presumably normal or successful Americans tend to be less apathetic and to find more meaning in existence than psychiatric patients.[52] Perhaps overcoming boredom and becoming "exuberant, enthusiastic" require reflection in order to discover a rationale for a way of living, to focus one's interests, and to evaluate rewarding and punishing experiences.

4. *Empathy or Sympathy.* Some persons experience vicariously the feelings and problems of other persons or groups (and sometimes even objects) and to "protect and help those who are vulnerable."[53] Items on a questionnaire include: "I feel very angry when I see someone being ill-treated"; "I become more irritated than sympathetic when I see someone's tears."[54] There may be little or no difference between persons from a different social classes in this respect, as was once demonstrated in a Finnish study.[55] Even though there may be a low relation between scales allegedly measuring the same "trait,"[56] perhaps reflection is required before the principal perceives and appreciates the plight of another person and, if need be, imagines how he himself would be affected if he were to be similarly disturbed or deprived.

5. *Types A and B.* Within recent years psychologists, psychiatrists, and others have found it useful and fruitful to classify persons into two types, called A and B, frequently on the basis of questionnaires, interviews, or close observations. In contrast with B's, A's tend to be more prone to suffer from coronary ailments and to alternate between "active-coping" and "giving up more frequently and intensely";[57] or to be more involved perhaps in competitive sports and other leisure activities.[58] The "vigorous" efforts of A's to master their environment may result either in success or failure and they may be more likely than B's to struggle impulsively and then, after failing, to reflect upon their actions. Perhaps A's gen-

erally hesitate less than B's; if so, here may be a "trait" that affects the consistency of such hesitation.

6. *Orientation.* This disposition, which merits slightly more extensive discussion than its five predecessors, refers to a principal's "generalized expectations" that are "contingent" upon his own behavior or are "controlled by forces outside himself and may occur independently of his own actions." The definition paraphrases slightly that of the psychologist whose widely-used questionnaire requires the subject to select from pairs of statements the alternative with which he agrees; for example:

1. When I make plans, I am almost certain that I can make them work.

2. It is not always wise to plan too far ahead because many things turn out to be a matter of good or bad fortune anyhow.[59]

Perhaps acquiring and then possessing an internal orientation (statement 1) requires more reflection than an external orientation (statement 2). The connection between the orientation and hesitation has not been firmly established, particularly among children,[60] but more compelling is its relation to actions possibly requiring varying degrees of hesitation. "Among Americans, with notable exceptions," according to a summary of four studies, "more internals than externals once tried to quit or reduce smoking after learning the dangers of the habit; more of the unmarried, sexually-engaged women used contraceptives; more of the husbands functioned more consistently and less aggressively toward their wives; more of the nurses were more satisfied with, and interested in their profession."[61]

The relations between impulsivity-reflection and those six dispositions is never astonishingly impressive. Sometimes, too, anticipated relations turn out to be abysmally low. Thus the relation between "nonplanning" (obtained from questioning German students about the ways in which they wrote term papers, went shopping, and similar actions) and impulsivity as measured by the Matching Test and a questionnaire turned out to be of little or no significance.[62] Or, you or I might guess that hesitating to engage in "novel or risky situations" might be a disposition that generalizes impulsivity to most situations so considered by principals; and yet that was once scarcely the case for Canadian students regarding their "willingness to taste unusual foods."[63] Obviously, caution is required.

In two domains of human activity, however, it seems more reasonable to assume that degrees of hesitation play a discernible role. First, since reflection requires the passing of time as measured by a clock and impulsivity the passing of relatively less time before the principal responds, it may be anticipated that the subjective passing of time may be related to hesitation.[64] In two studies the experimental subjects (adolescents consisting of delinquents, psychiatric patients, and normal controls) were instructed to reproduce temporal intervals ranging from one second to four minutes. With an exception, there was a pronounced tendency for those classified as impulsive on the Matching Test and another standardized test to underproduce the intervals and for reflective subjects to overproduce them. Associated with impulsivity, therefore, was a tendency for subjective time to pass more slowly and hence for perceived intervals to appear longer than clock time, although, in fact, they were shorter. The exception, with one but not with another method of measuring hesitation, impulsivity was not related to the underestimation of ten seconds or less. In addition, the highly impulsive individuals tended to make less accurate temporal judgments than did their less impulsive peers. Shaky evidence suggests that the temporal inaccuracies of the impulsive subjects increased as the laboratory tasks became more complicated. Impulsive principals seemed more willing to predict future events, possibly because they were more prone to take risks.[65]

The other domain is that of age: do tendencies to be impulsive or reflective change as individuals grow older? One review of the experimental literature based almost exclusively on the Matching Test suggests that with increasing age American children become more reflective and hence, in the sense that they are more capable of delaying their responses, less impulsive.[66] Fifth graders characterized as impulsive on that Test, for example, tended to select stereotyped but incorrect associations to words (*"Blue* is to *color* as *sad* is to *happy* rather than *mood*); but, the difference in Grade 5 tended to diminish.[67] At "around 10 years of age," such children become "maximally aware of the speed-accuracy tradeoff":[68] greater haste makes greater waste because there is less time to reflect. But another review of nine studies using the identical test revealed a decrease in the number of errors with an increase in age but no "dramatic" increase in response time.[69] In a longitudinal study in which older children between the ages of 11 and 14 were assessed on versions of the Matching Test, "moderate stability" of scores rather than change seemed evident;[70] possibly the stability was greater for the error than response-time scores on the same test for children at the ages of 3, 4, 5, and 11, which suggests that a "competency" factor may also have been involved.[71] Likewise, samples of British children between the ages of 7 and 15 revealed only "slight" differences with increasing age;[72] and an investigation in Sweden reports "no marked differences in adults ranging in age from 20 to 65.[73]

In evaluating the somewhat muddled results from studies on age, it must be remembered that in general "children need more time to execute processes than do adults"[74] and therefore a portion of their hesitation may involve not reflection concerning Critical Questions but may be due to limiting experience or even physical or physiological processes. On the Matching Test and with an impressively large number of children between the ages of five and ten, it was once shown that samples of American, Japanese, and Israeli children responded somewhat differently at different ages, conceivably but not definitely to be explained by differences in the ways the written languages appear (phonetic or partially symbolic like the variants on the test) or by the varying anxiety accompanying the performance of tasks in the three societies.[75] In addition, even as alcohol by itself may not conventionally reduce stress unless the individual engages in a somewhat challenging task while intoxicated,[76] so age probably interacts with other factors in the principal's milieu or personal-

ity. For age, then, once more the reflective conclusion must
be a guess: As a result of the restricting, regulatory requirements of socialization systems in every society it seems likely
that at least during childhood reflection rather than immediate impulse satisfaction increases; yet there is the possibility that only reflection and not impulsivity is related to age.[77]

In spite of the not always consistent findings reported in
this section, one generalization emerges: degrees of hesitation are embedded in the personalities of principals and so,
even as personalities vary, so must the consequences for hesitation.

Self

Any organism, especially a human being, is perpetually reacting to events that are external or internal. Whether or not
hesitation is a "trait," there is an enduring core to which he
may refer his actions and which also affects those actions.
That core is the self that functions as a critical observer of
what transpires. Once again eye-blinkings: I blinked when
the bright light reached my eye; I did not decide to blink;
not I but me just blinked. The principal may also have a
similar view of what appears to be an event within himself:
I did it, I just did it, and I am proud of myself. Around that
self are collected conscious memories, values, and moral
judgments.

We are concerned here not with a metaphysical but with
a real, experienced entity. American children, when given the
simple challenge, "Tell us about yourself," have been able to
respond, and many do so in terms of height, weight, hair and
eye color, ethnicity, gender, and a host of other attributes.[78]
College students use subtler categories to describe themselves and may be able to do so relatively consistently over
time.[79] Perhaps, "subjective thoughts and feelings" are considered to be more diagnostic of "the inner or real self" than
actual behavior; American students may praise their subjective selves because their mode of assessment has been affected by widespread psychoanalytic thinking which stresses

the importance of subjective musings and impulses.[80] In fact, the self-esteem of black American high school students was once shown to be related to their academic performance: the lower the performance, the lower the self-esteem tended to be.[81] Similarly, the self-esteem of white South African adolescent girls—as well as their self-perceived ability—was related to their educational and vocational aspirations.[82] It is the self, then, that raises or does not raise the Critical Questions and hence affects the degree and mode of hesitation.

To affect degrees of hesitation, the self must be salient. According to an Australian psychologist, "the greater the confusion (sense of uncertainty, bafflement, or frustration) in the course of a thought or an action sequence, the more likely it is that imagery will be aroused and the more vivid it will be."[83] Such imagery is likely to be examined, to produce increased hesitation, and eventually to be referred to the self before it subsides. You probably react differently to questions concerning issues such as capital punishment, abortion, or nuclear freeze when you reply abstractly from the way you do when you apply the problem to yourself or to someone who is important to you. You must reflect even more when you approach the question abstractly or morally. Even seeing oneself in a mirror under some circumstances may possibly increase self-awareness and affect ongoing activity;[84] and being critically evaluated may produce the hesitation accompanying shyness, anxiety, and finding "an excuse for poor performance."[85] If it be true that rewards administered by the self are of greater interest than those allocated by external agents,[86] then such judgments must involve greater hesitation regarding anticipated satisfaction, inhibition, guilt, or feelings of freedom. Self-monitoring, in short, requires the principal to reflect in order to relate what has happened or is going to happen to that self (Route 1b); but such hesitation may be diminished if the self has been previously involved in a similar issue or problem (Route 3a).

We can remove self-monitoring from a metaphysical realm by considering two items on a "test" designed to tap that tendency among American students:

I have trouble changing my behavior to suit different people and different situations.

If someone is lying to me, I usually know it at once from that person's manner or expression.[87]

In the first instance, the subject must hesitate to ascertain how he can "suit" the people and situations; in the second, he is so concerned about the someone's relation to himself that he hesitates to decide whether he is confronted with a liar. A summary of experimental studies suggests that "individuals show heightened sensitivity to self-related stimuli," that their "predictions, attributions, and inferences" tend to be "more confident" when they are "in the self-relevant domains."[88] At times stimuli can become "self-related" or consistent only when the information principals already possess is made salient by another person, the so-called Socratic effect:[89] don't you realize that this is contrary to your religious belief?

The degree of self-monitoring in turn is affected by self-esteem, the internal feelings the individual has about his self. To retain faith in religious doctrines and not to backslide, one theologian believes, the individual must relate the doctrines not only to a forgiving God but also to his own persevering self.[90] According to a competent summary of what is known about this feeling, the principal receives information related to the esteem in which he is held by other people, or in which he believes he is held; such feedback must be judged and evaluated so that some hesitation is essential. Self-esteem in American society may be lowered as a result of minority status, aging, receiving essential assistance from one's peers, and other personal relations; and a lowering of self-esteem may produce less interest in self-control.[91] From another viewpoint, self-esteem is closely involved in face-saving: the principal hesitates longer when he feels he cannot meet "essential requirements placed upon him by virtue of the position he occupies,"[92] especially perhaps if he is a Type A person who finds himself in an aversive and uncontrollable situation.[93]

The concept of self-control is favored by parents, psychia-

PERSONALITY 81

trists, and others who administer rules of conduct, namely, "a person's regulation of his own or her own psychological, behavioral, and physical processes."[94] Self-control and the ensuing hesitation require the postponement of reward and often additional reflection concerning the value of the momentary sacrifice. Principals may lose control without realizing that they are responding impulsively at a given moment or over time. In Western societies, for example, it is easy to relax as one receives news on the radio or television and thus, since the motive for listening or viewing may not be to be informed, unwittingly a version of the news is thereby absorbed. An analysis of Canadian news once indicated that the principals were likely to obtain a superficial, incomplete, or distorted view of events associated with crime unless they paused, hesitated, and sought to discover or imagine the actual facts behind the snippets being communicated to them.[95] In addition, viewers may not be aware of the amount of violence they are witnessing on television since only a careful, objective analysis of its content can reveal the precise number of programs or the frequency or rate of violence in each program;[96] and the ultimate effect of witnessing TV violence on audiences is difficult to ascertain. To be sure, viewers, listeners, and readers may believe they have not relinquished control because they themselves have decided to expose themselves to those media. But do they really decide one must ask, in view of the pressures exerted upon them from early childhood and especially as adults?

Throughout this chapter the effects of personality have been portrayed as a precarious enterprise. Some of this variability must be traced to the moods of the self: "one's general state of being over a limited period of time; hours or days but probably not weeks and certainly not months or years."[97] The artificial induction of a mood by having American students in an experiment read rational or irrational statements, such as "It is a terrible catastrophe when things are not as one wants them to be"[98] or by having children describe circumstances that had made them happy or sad[99] may tend to affect their judgments and behavior. After a rugby match, more Australian spectators whose team had been defeated than those whose team had won forwarded letters that they thought had been lost but that had been secretly placed on the windshield wipers of a sample of cars plastered with symbols indicating the team supported by the occupants.[100] Presumably the decision to be altruistic or not by extending such trivial help to an unknown stranger resulted not from profound reflection, but from the mood induced by the game. Details of events that "match" the principal's mood or emotional state are likely to be more efficiently retained in the absence of such matching, and recall may be improved when the individual's momentary mood resembles somewhat his emotional state during the original learning.[101] The mood at a given moment, consequently, may affect what is perceived, the biases being evoked, and the learning process. On a simple physiological level, the performance of principals—such as answering a telephone bell or solving arithmetic problems—may vary with the length of time they have been asleep as well as the phase of sleep from which they have been awakened.[102] Simply hearing background music may produce a mood change.[103] We cannot specify, however, the direct effect of any mood as such upon degrees of hesitation unless the process thus affected is also known; thus if the mood creates momentary uncertainty, which may stimulate the quest for additional information,[104] then perhaps greater hesitation is the consequence. Are you, or are you not, a moody person? If you are, then perhaps you and the rest of us find it difficult to anticipate whether you will hesitate to reach a decision until we and you have first determined your mood at the moment you are perplexed.

IN SHORT: perhaps remarkably, the principal—his personality, often his self—though always influenced by his culture and society, has unique experiences in the present or past that facilitate or inhibit tendencies to hesitate and hence to be or not to be impulsive or reflective; consequently in most moods he is able to assess his own potentialities, anticipations, and other Critical Questions before passing judgment and reacting.

5

Other Persons

Nobody, not even a hermit, would dare deny that other persons have constant and profound effects upon the judgments and actions of principals. An individual who places emphasis upon self-monitoring is said to be "particularly sensitive to the expression and self-presentation of others in social situations and uses these as guidelines for monitoring and managing his own self-presentation and expressive behavior."[1] One of the items employed conventionally to determine self-monitoring is the following: "In a group I am rarely the center of attention."[2] Sociologists frequently pay tribute to what are sometimes called reference groups whose values—and encouragements and restraints—principals emulate as they strive to achieve varied goals or to pass judgments upon themselves. The group may be the one to which the individual himself belongs such as his family, neighborhood, and nation. Or, it may be a group which he aspires to join and whose values or behavior he holds in high esteem.[3] A principal's self-esteem may thus depend on the group with which he compares himself; for example, it was once shown that individual blacks in South Africa felt "relatively more deprived" vis-á-vis whites (English- and Afrikaans-speakers), so called-Coloreds, and Indians than they did with reference to their own ethnic group.[4]

To assess the effect of other persons on the individual's degree of hesitation, then, two foreground problems must be analyzed. The first concerns the characteristics attributed to the other person by the principal: does he consider him a friend, a stranger, or an enemy? The second focuses upon the possible effects of the attribution: if he comes from a friendly country, should I trust him? Indeed most, but not all events are related to other persons, so that principals seek to understand the past, the present, and the future by concentrating upon the dramatis personae.[5] Those other persons, moreover, are judged by the principal "on the basis of the kind of object he is to himself."[6] The self plays a role.

Attribution

Under most circumstances the presence or absence of another being is perceived with little hesitation. That person or group is visible, audible, or stimulating one of the other senses, unless he, she, or they are mistaken for an animal, a plant, or an object. Recognition is followed by attribution, a process requiring varying degrees of hesitation. An acquaintance approaches you. Before noticing him, other people may have moved in your direction, but you have ignored them; no, not exactly ignored, because without reflection you have noted that they were strangers and only passing by without bumping into you. If that person is your dearly beloved mother and you have not been separated from her since infancy, you know who she is and, unless you are in a grouchy mood, with almost no hesitation your affection for her—positive, negative, or in-between—becomes salient; yet you may hesitate a trifle more as you wonder how or why she happens to be walking on that street at that particular time. But suppose a stranger stops you and simply asks for directions to a particular place, does the time you devote to answering this simple request depend upon how you immediately categorize him on the basis of his clothing and the social status of the location he is seeking?[7] Or, a crowd of persons converges at one point ahead of you: do you wonder what is happening, do you reflect in order to decide what they are doing or whether it is safe for you to walk toward them? Judgments of other persons, in short, may be effortless or demand reflection. However small or great, the effort requires projecting some attribution on to the other person or group.

Attribution can be speedy with little reflection when that other person or group is familiar or when it evokes familiar responses: "greater attention and processing"—and hence greater hesitation—are likely to be devoted to "relatively infrequent" actions than to behavior that is ordinarily anticipated.[8] Events, including the individuals and groups therein, are almost infinitely complicated from someone's viewpoint. You see a flag. That event can be appraised most variously: the chemist may appraise its constituents, the physicist the light waves reaching one's retina, the physiologist the reaction of the eye's rods and cones, and so on. But you may pay no attention to these relevant details, you note the flag and, if anyone questions you, that is all you report. Like the flag your perception and assessment of the other person or group may be equally stereotyped, so that little hesitation is required before passing judgment. Generally, consequently, the principal is provided with more information than he can efficiently encode, so that he perceives and pays attention only to those segments he can comprehend or utilize.[9] Stereotypes enable him quickly and even impulsively to perceive and act upon confirming evidence, especially that pertaining to or emanating from the appearance, gender, distinctive attributes, and general or specific reputation of the other persons.[10] At a glance, stereotypes convey the information he thinks he requires with little or no hesitation.

Slightly greater hesitation may be required when the principal must persuade himself that he has insight into the beliefs and feelings of the group in which he is participating. If he would not be conspicuous, and if he would consciously or unconsciously avoid reflection, he may induce within himself an "impression of universality": he may sincerely believe that other persons are similarly reacting to the events he himself is perceiving.[11] By means of such projection human beings "learn to read the silent communications" of the space and contact between themselves and others, so that they know quickly the proper amount to tolerate or provide; each principal has his own code that varies from society to society.[12] You know with little hesitation whom you may kiss and from whom you may expect a kiss; and you also know how physically close or distant you will be when you converse with a stranger or a friend, other matters and contingencies being equal. In addition after an action has occurred, the principal may easily provide the explanation he might have been able to offer if he had reflected beforehand; thus American men may cross a street more slowly when an attractive rather than an unattractive young woman invades their personal space without deliberately making that decision, but they may later be able to indicate their feelings at the time.[13]

A significant attitude affecting behavior is the principal's trust in the other person. "Parents usually can be relied upon to keep their promises"; "Most elected public officials are really sincere in their campaign promises"—those are two items on a scale once administered to American students to measure their "interpersonal trust."[14] When such trust exists as a result of past experience, there need be little hesitation concerning how that other person should be treated or appraised (Route 3a).

What explanation is given for the behavior of another person or group? Principals may be eager to supply a ready explanation, but sometimes they are as baffled as psychologists and other observers who would offer their hypotheses (variable linkage). Two factors interact: the personality of the principal and the situation. If a person's residence catches fire, he flees; the situation is the causative factor. If the murderer has a pathological urge to kill, the explanation is to be found primarily in him and not in his victim. Although such circumstances are obvious at the extreme ends of a continuum, more usually the principal must hesitate before deciding whether the other person's behavior can be attributed to his personality, the requirements of the situation, or a combination of both. Ordinarily you believe that man is honest, but on this occasion the temptation was too great. In spite of the depression and other hardships they are experiencing, an observing if not observant journalist anticipates, perhaps without documentation, that the people of a country will remain cheerful and even optimistic.

Comparable evidence, though largely of the conventional sort, suggests quite tentatively and with numerous exceptions that principals tend to attribute their own behavior to events and environmental circumstances and the behavior of other persons to their own stable dispositions, their traits. In either case, however, they may place greater emphasis on traits than external factors as causal explanations; and they may also ascribe their successes to their own ability and their failures to those external factors.[15] If this be so, then judging others may require more hesitation than judging oneself, and judging one's failure more than one's successes: personality dispositions must be conceived and require reflection before becoming salient as explanations, whereas events may or must be perceived with less reflection. A temporal factor also affects hesitation: possibly a dispositional rather than a situational explanation tends to be employed more readily for future than past behavior,[16] inasmuch as the informant may have more confidence in a more or less known person than somewhat unpredictable events in the future. Attributions to personality may possibly endure longer than those ascribed to situations and thus eventually over time require less hesitation.[17] If the principal's attribution is an internal disposition, he may also evaluate the disposition as being, for example, egotistic or self-effacing;[18] yet situations may be but are not always assessed less subjectively. Generalizations again are difficult because individuals devote varying amounts of time and effort to try to understand themselves and others.

Principals differ concerning their inclination to use personality or situations as their attributional explanation, whether or not they follow the modal tendencies of their peers. Perhaps, as one investigator has suggested, they generally follow the "rule" of first using personality for purposes of attribution and then, if need be, of "subtracting" the situation from that attribution to arrive at a judgment; thus the personality factor may loom large when and if the person being judged does not appear to conform to the norm required by the situation. A child who misbehaves in school is aberrant in that situation and consequently the explanation is sought within him. Again, however, the particular principals and the situations must be taken into account. Young children may increasingly select friends on the basis of their attributed characteristics, whereas their use of situational behavior as the criterion may tend to remain more or less constant; and when they compare themselves with others, they may use models similar to themselves, or so they believe.[19] But experiences shared in similar situations can also produce friendliness and feelings of similarity with little hesitation. For example, when Soviet veterans from the Afghanistan war and American veterans from the Vietnam war met in Moscow in 1988, they apparently could not speak each other's languages, but that "barrier seemed to matter little. Before a translation was complete, the others were nodding their heads in understanding, or reaching their arms across the tables in an embrace." A young Soviet student exclaimed, "I have friends I have never spoken to like this. But these guys, they are like my brothers. They know."[20]

Judgment concerning the political roles of personalities may be made impulsively when the appearance of a candidate or a leader or one of his demonstrated characteristics is appealing or repulsive. Attributions then are not essential as the person being judged blatantly or subtly expresses his own viewpoint. The principle of one-man-one-vote, for example, has been perceived differently by many Afrikaners from the way it has been approved by most blacks in South Africa. The former have believed that, although they are in the minority, they have been better qualified to vote and would lose their privileges and their nation its social and economic achievements if the principle were followed, whereas the latter have subscribed to the principle that requires the transfer of power to themselves. In contrast the same principle has been utilized in the divided Cyprus. There the Greek Cypriots in the majority have wished the majority to rule, but the Turkish Cypriots in the minority have claimed that the principle violated their rights and deprived them of equal status and privileges.[21]

Effects

After indicating that the goals, attitudes, intentions, and feelings attributed to the other person or group of persons may affect the principal's judgments and actions, it is necessary to flip the coin and consider the effect of others upon principals, either proactively or retroactively. These effects include not only the resulting attributions but also changes that may occur regardless of the attribution. Long-run consequences of others may be particularly compelling. A group of psychiatrists once examined 130 patients suffering from symptoms of uncontrollable impulsivity that included "fears of going out of control and injuring someone, homicidal ideation, repetitive aggressive behavior under the influence of alcohol." These persons, who tended to be lower-middle class in status, revealed "childhood deprivations" resulting from home conditions that had been "very tenuous and emotionally impoverished."[22] The deprivation and the conditions had been created by other persons and apparently induced the lasting effects. A moment's pause: Other persons must have been responsible for the patients' parents; and still others for the patients' parents' parents; how far back must one go in posing the Critical Questions? A simpler, though annoying post hoc degree of hesitation must also occur when the principal is asked, in the words of one study, "Were there things that you would have liked to have said or done during the session but did not? What kept you from doing those things?"[23]

Short-term effects of other persons are too numerous to categorize. Consider first a dramatic, tragic illustration. In 1985 a young, well-educated member of a black opposition group in South Africa, the African National Congress, planted a mine in a shopping center that killed five persons and injured forty-eight others; subsequently he was found guilty and hanged. At his trial he never denied that he was responsible for the criminal action, he said that setting off the bomb was to be a protest against the murder of Africans by the armed forces but that he intended to avoid killing anyone. He planted the bomb, which would go off in thirty minutes, and hurried to the telephone office to issue a warning to the center concerning the pending explosion. That office was approximately five minutes away from the center. He discovered all five telephones were in use. Why didn't he interrupt one of the speakers and ask to use the phone? We can only guess that he rejected the possibility, whether or not he attributed hostility to those speakers and assumed that his urgent request would be rejected. In any case, he waited "about fifteen minutes" and, according to his testimony, he believed that a warning then or later would create confusion at the center and even more people would be killed. He "didn't think of going back" to the center, he stated, and the mine exploded.[24] Thus the unpredicted, fortuitous presence of the other persons at the telephones disrupted the man's well-considered plan, evoked attributions preventing him from interrupting them, caused him with little hesitation to flee, and produced the tragedy for those killed and wounded and for himself.

Most of us can think of interpersonal relations in which the effect of other persons is difficult to anticipate. Probably, no possibly, as has once been demonstrated, principals find that a large group provides a "more impoverishing and alienating environment" for themselves than do small groups;[25] if so, their degree of hesitation may be greater as numbers increase. A psychologist has listed a baker's-two-dozen illustrations of "interactions where the question of predictability is psychologically problematic." They include "an analyst and patient," "labor and management negotiations," "political candidates and voters," "boxers," "couples in courtship," and "children playing hide-and-seek."[26] With the exception of the extreme situations already mentioned—the other person suddenly flashes a bright light or makes a loud noise—it is difficult to imagine *precisely* how another person will affect a principal. As an inmate holds a gun and threatens to shoot the guards unless they allow him to escape, will some guards hesitate and reflect concerning the possibility of overpowering the man or call what they believe to be his bluff? A lover protests his devotion to the other person; will the beloved's momentary mood or health affect the reciprocal protestation? There may be a tendency for principals to conform and accept the prevailing view or orders of other persons, especially those in authority, but it is clear that both figuratively and literally some soldiers refuse to obey orders to massacre presumably innocent civilians as occurred in the My Lai incident during the Vietnam War.[27]

One might suppose that, when the other person is a hypnotist, he can induce the principal to react with almost the minimum of hesitation. As one serious, competent investigator has written, however, "the data of hypnosis have proved so puzzling." The hypnotized person, according to one view, may be genuinely hypnotized or only be enacting the role he has come to believe to be associated with hypnosis. In comparison with "normal" conditions, during the "trance" he probably initiates fewer or no actions, is more suggestible, and is more subject to amnesia and agnosia; and he also executes commands or suggestions post-hypnotically without ostensibly being aware of their origin within the previous "trance."[28]

Social psychologists have attempted to discover some regularity resulting from the presence of other persons by devising conventional experimental and therefore artificial situations in which the performance of the usual subjects is compared with behaving alone or in the presence of others. Generally the measures are the speed and accuracy with which laboratory tasks are performed. By and large the expectation that performance would be affected has not been powerfully vindicated. A careful analysis of 241 studies suggests that not only may the impairment of performance on "complex" tasks as well as on less complex ones be "small," but also in some instances that performance can be not damaged but facilitated.[29]

The effect of the other person is more predictable when his behavior or role is influenced by cultural rules known to the principal. Literal or metaphorical distance serves as an excellent illustration. When an individual's "personal space" is invaded—the person with whom he is speaking comes too close from his standpoint—he may either move a bit or feel uncomfortable with little or no reflection.[30] Not surprisingly it has been noted that friends approach one another more closely than strangers.[31] And, of course, in Western society a married pair discuss topics of interest to themselves which they would not mention to outsiders; but they hesitate longer to do so when the relationship is clouded. It is probably true that the presence of other persons provokes some responses not only because they occupy a certain space and because their very presence is stimulating but also because their number (a single individual, a group, a crowd) may be judged satisfactory or unsatisfactory;[32] hence the principal may feel impelled to decide whether he feels comfortable or uncomfortable and whether he should remain in the situation or leave. Do you like large or small gatherings?

Social requirements fluctuate from group to group. The first bit of "homework" in a Peace Corps manual on learning the Somali language is straightforward: "Shake hands with your instructors at least three times between now and the next time the class meets." But immediately a warning is issued: "Do not attempt to learn to hold on to an American's hand as long as you would a Somali's."[33] The stranger in Somali society must learn to reflect concerning the duration of a handshake there but must not acquire that group's rule or obligation among Americans; handshaking for the time being requires reflection.

Longstanding beliefs in a society, especially those transmitted to children and others without relevant experience, are likely to be accepted with little hesitation because of a conviction that the older or more competent persons are correct and must be obeyed (Route 3a). In the West there is a widespread belief among all kinds of people, whether alcoholics or not, that drinking alcohol reduces tension. This view is supported by some, not by all systematic evidence collected under controlled conditions, but it seems reasonably clear that "the belief that alcohol has been consumed can exert a greater influence on behavior than the pharmacological impact of ethanol," at least when the alcoholic content in the blood stream is low.[34]

Differences in social or economic status within a society necessarily induce upper and lower status individuals to judge and plan their own actions to conform somewhat to their conception of the other group and hence to reflect concerning their goals and values. Those considering themselves inferior to others may be motivated to improve their own lot, even though they are in a superior position with reference to still other persons. In spite of the fact that their income may be sufficient and higher than that of many of their immediate associates, they may still wish an income comparable to the wealthiest group in the community. "Relative deprivation" thus occurs when the principal has not reached a goal that he himself seeks, when he compares his situation with that of other persons, and when he also believes it is "feasible", or just, for him to attain a condition comparable to theirs.[35] To make the comparison, reflection is required at the outset and then continually.

The very anticipation of contact with a group may affect a principal's reactions and hence the degree to which he hesitates before judging or behaving. Acceptance or rejection, joy or sorrow, stability or change can be expected, so that some reflection may be necessary to be able to make a choice. In one experiment, American adults functioned as jurors in a simulated trial portrayed to them on a videotape: one group was videotaped during the "trial" and was told that their reactions were being recorded for use in an experiment; the control group was not given that message and no camera was pointed at them. During and after the showing or non-showing of the videotape they were asked to recall the details of what they had been witnessing. The presence of the TV camera impaired recall only at the outset; later the recall of the two groups did not differ, except that ostensibly being recorded by this popular medium affected somewhat adversely those low in "public consciousness" (measured by a paper-and-pencil questionnaire referring to concern for one's appearance, behavior, and self-presentation). Also the camera had no effect upon the verdict rendered by the subjects, or upon their ratings of the different "witnesses."[36] In this instance—and the example has been deliberately selected in order to provoke hesitation concerning the generalization at the outset of the paragraph—the anticipation of providing a TV record for other persons had only a very brief effect.

The effects of other persons are subject to change as a result of experience; background factors come to the fore. Initial mistrust requiring reflection before the principal is willing to act can give way to trust and little hesitation (Route 3a). In contrast, an unfavorable experience can reverse the process so that the principal thereafter hesitates longer before reacting.

Silence and Lying

Silence and lying are paired here and in the real world because they are both ways of coping with other persons, silence ostensibly by contributing no information, lying by providing false information. Of course, there can be considerable overlap between the two. The principal who is silent gives the wrong impression that he has nothing to say or that he would thus express his disdain, neither of which may be true; or he is silent in order to express that disdain quite eloquently. Does or does he not lie not only by telling untruths but also by being silent concerning real truths? In either case the decision to be silent or to lie may stem from prior reflection concerning what the individual wishes to communicate (Routes 3a and 3b).

When a principal is asked a question and does not reply or when he suddenly stops speaking, consequently, the explanation for his silence is varied. He may be generally or specifically stupid; he may have nothing to say. Perhaps he cannot complete his own sentence, or he must grope for a verbal expression. He may hesitate and then decide to employ silence as a form of communication. For some good reason he feels that it would be unwise or inappropriate to speak out. Silence then becomes a form of communication: the silent one signifies non-cooperation with other persons or thus expresses hostility toward them. It is said—by whom?—that

at precious moments two persons deeply in love may hesitate to speak for fear that breaking the silence will interrupt
or disrupt their feelings. In "Eastern thought," and among
Quakers, silence is part of a ritual; in the West a moment or
more of silence at a specified time may be an expression of
respect for a departed hero or loved one.[37] In this context
silence forces or enables principals to reflect and becomes a
cause rather than a consequence of reflection.

For the observer the silence of the principal may be difficult to interpret (variable linkage). From his standpoint silence that exceeds what he believes to be a normal delay he
may interpret as hesitation, regardless of whatever motives
he attributes to the principal or the explanation he attaches
thereto. Thus a silent person may seem to be hesitating in
order to withhold information or not to be impulsive when
in fact he is reflecting in order to solve a problem or reach a
decision before continuing to speak or write. Metaphors may
be employed and so there are "nations that seem to slumber
in silence for long centuries." Here presumably no specific
reference is being made to hesitation, only to the absence of
communication or action from the writer's historical standpoint. Another cosmic truth: "Nothing has changed the nature of man so much as the loss of silence." That statement
implies that we poor human beings no longer reflect as much
as we allegedly once did. The compiler of the quotations above
also suggests that modern mass communications, being per-
vasive, may diminish the periods of silence for their audiences,[38] presumably because they provide ready-made answers and hence promote less hesitation and especially less
reflection.

A Christian clergyman has devoted a whole book to praising silence. He notes at the outset this gem from Euripides:
"Our miseries do not spring / From houses wanting locks
and bolts / But from unbridled tongues." He believes that
"there are some things better expressed by silence than by
speech" and he recalls what he considers to be the wisdom
of proverbs such as "brevity is the soul of wit" and "empty
vessels make the greatest sound." "Some things," he therefore thinks, "are better expressed by silence than by speech,"

such as the "symbolic messages concerning the silent dead" that can be found in churchyards. Jesus himself, he believes, provided "the great model of silence."[39] Silence can thus be a positive achievement because action thereafter stems from profound reflection. But suppose the principal does not reflect as he silently hesitates?

Related to silence, especially when the principal is alone, is solitude that may be deliberately or unwittingly sought: the principal is silent and his contemporaries, being absent, are for him perforce also silent. In Western society solitude may occur involuntarily under adverse circumstances, particularly when the principal is unable to control events. The child is an orphan, he is younger than his siblings, he has parents who are divorced, he has been hospitalized. Or the adult is ill, belongs to a minority or immigrant group, or is widowed. Discomfort results and misery permeates reflection, even when occasionally "aloneness" turns out to be "a healing experience."[40] A loneliness scale has been devised that includes items such as "I lack companionship," "No one really knows me well."[41] American students' scores on that scale were once found to be related somewhat but not impressively to other paper-and-pencil measures: positively to self-labelling concerning loneliness, depression, and anxiety; and negatively to self-esteem, extraversion, affiliative tendencies, and assertiveness.[42]

Solitude achieved by pairs or by individuals with common philosophies, however, may be "vivifying" and create a sense of freedom.[43] Such persons thus avoid stimulation and distraction, they may relax and then perhaps reflect without interruption. We know, I think, that religious figures such as Jesus, Mohammed, and Buddha received their visions and insights when totally alone; that hermits have been encouraged especially in the early years of Christianity. In the Roman Empire, according to one scholar, some members of the ruling classes owned farms outside cities; they as well as early Christians retreated to hermitages and monasteries; at least in retrospect the retreats have been considered to be "more harmonious communities than the society" that was therefore being abandoned. The same writer finds "a direct relationship" between "the vision of solitude in society and the evolution of advanced capitalism."[44] Here and also in connection with the loneliness scale mentioned above, it is impossible to declare whether principals hesitate and consequently seek solitude or are lonely, or whether solitude and loneliness facilitate hesitation and reflection.

Lying, deliberately not telling and hence being silent concerning the truth—whatever truth is—implies that another person is the recipient, although wittingly or unwittingly the principal may lie to himself. More often than not, lying requires some hesitation in order to distort the truth; you have to reflect a bit to tell a convincing whopper. Some psychiatrists and psychologists consider lying a significant symptom or tendency within the individual. They suggest that the ability to tell a lie may be a sign of growth among young children since "falsehood is impossible until the notion of a word transcendent to oneself is recognized."[45] What are branded lies by the observers may result from the principals' failure to remember the truth concerning past events, so that their reflection leads to inaccurate judgments. Otherwise lying may serve important functions in interacting with other persons: the principal thereby manipulates them to achieve his goal, he makes a favorable impression, or he avoids responsibility for his own action. Think of the lies or partial lies told by many salesmen if they are to be successful, lies either from the viewpoint of a neutral observer or even of themselves. Consider the need for secrecy in planning the strategies or tactics to be employed in sporting events or in preparing for and fighting wars: the principal deliberately misleads his adversaries by being silent or by communicating false information. A criminal may seek to avoid detection by adopting a different name, by changing his appearance or residence, or by assuming a new role in society; if brought to trial, he may deliberately lie or, in the United States, invoke the Fifth Amendment that permits him to be silent and not offer evidence against himself. Ingratiation to win the affection of another person or to gain favors from him or her demands some reflective planning before the role can be convincingly performed; or more or less spontaneous lies can be scattered in the midst of a conversation or social event.[46]

It is undoubtedly true, as a French psychiatrist has suggested, that "not everyone lies with the same facility or the same ability." He adds that "the true mythomaniac constructs a coherent story (coherent for himself at least) that he tries to make others believe. He ends by believing in his own fabrication, and this is the measure that those around him believe it."[47] Even pathological liars may hesitate a bit before coining a distortion, but over time they can become practitioners of the art and hence hesitate less as they overcome moral scruples. When the principal lies to himself, he may be bolstering his self-esteem, rationalizing his misdeeds, or protecting values he allegedly holds dear; here the mask requires reflection to construct but, after completion, it reduces hesitation by its very availability. After a principal upon reflection decides to lie, he may or may not experience guilt. If he does feel guilty, he notes whether he has violated his own expectations or those of the lie's recipient or of peers generally. The principal's audience may expect him to share their viewpoint by lying or they in turn may lie when they claim to believe him.

Deliberate lying involves moral issues and hence a reference to Critical Questions. Games and wars must be won, but at what cost? In a literal sense scientists lie whenever they use a placebo while conducting experiments with human beings. To isolate the effects of a drug upon experimental subjects, for example, it is necessary to have a control group of persons who do not receive the drug but who believe that they do as they are given the placebo. Here the end, really testing the drug, justifies the deceiving procedure, but the experimenters may have to hesitate more than a trifle when they consider that they are depriving the controls of the possible benefits from the drugs. Novelists and dramatists obviously lie in a literal sense when they strive to have their characters and situations appear "real" to their readers and audiences who are likely to be critical in a negative sense if the make-believe lie is not convincing or in accord with their experience or bias. But what about young children who cannot always make the distinction between the author's fantasy and reality? And of all the news that's fit to communicate in any mass medium, do or can we hesitate long enough to distinguish truth from deliberate or inadvertent falsehood?

Sometimes an untruth is so blatant that the observer can perceive the falsity with little reflection. In the last century a journalist writing from a canyon in the mining frontier of California reported at the beginning of an article: "The wind here is a holy terror to people who were raised in a dead calm. A puff will turn a dog inside out, and several stage companies have been busted by trying to keep paint on their wagons."[48] Obviously truth was not being communicated but presumably readers could immediately, with little hesitation, recognize that the white lies were conveying information about strong winds. Reflection was not needed, the impulsive reaction right now was to laugh or smile while acquiring exaggerated but relevant information about the winds in the canyon.

How can you as an observer tell when someone is lying? You may have what you consider facts that disprove what he says, facts that you yourself have gathered or that you obtain from others whom you trust. Or what he says you know or believe to be contrary to accepted facts or theories. But what do you do when you have no facts or theories and you have only the principal with whom to deal? Perhaps the observer under these circumstances notes whether that principal blushes or replies promptly to a relevant question. The validity of such impressions, moreover, is open to question; when pausing the principal may be reflecting in order to convey either an accurate or inaccurate communication. The device known as the lie detector (sometimes called a polygraph which is the recording instrument) does not concentrate upon the individual's reaction time, rather it enables the investigator to record differences in blood pressure, pulse, respiration, and skin temperature and conductivity when key and irrelevant questions are asked. These physiological responses are largely controlled by the autonomic nervous system and cannot be "voluntarily" manipulated by the individual. It has been estimated that skillful operators of this instrument have identified about three-quarters of suspected criminals as liars or truthful persons. The wrong diagnoses result from the fact that the principal's autonomic system may be affected not only by his desire to withhold the truth if he is guilty or to be alert if he is innocent, but also by his emotional tension, physiological abnormalities such as heart disease, mental abnormality, and "observed muscular movements which produce ambiguities or misleading indications in the blood pressure tracing." In some instances the lying or guilty person may be able to control these "involuntary" responses: his misleading response may result from his own prior "rationalization" of the crime or of the deed in question so that he is not disturbed by the crucial questions. In short, "It is a fact, of course, that some persons are better liars than others."[49]

IN SHORT: most relevantly, the principal's judgments and actions stem not only from his culture and society, his personality, and his previous experiences, but also from other persons who are present or have played or are likely to play a role in his existence; it is they, too, who affect his silences, his possible quest for solitude, his inclination to lie, and hence the degree of his hesitation.

6

Situations

Again and again the judgment and behavior of principals cannot be predicted because, as is stated, "it all depends." On what does it depend? Mood certainly plays a role as does the personality of a particular principal when the observer is unacquainted with him. Since the best-laid hypotheses of both principals and observers gang aft a-glay, it is little wonder that the goal of understanding and control of human behavior is often greeted with skepticism. As already noted especially in the last chapter, however, predictability can improve when the variable of situation is taken into account. A stutterer may bring his disposition to hesitate to all situations, but he is more likely to exhibit such hesitancy when a situation engenders anxiety;[1] in what situations will he be anxious?

Infinite are the situations in which human beings find themselves. They vary from a quiet sunset to an atomic explosion, from the silence of a monastery to the cries of a revolutionary crowd, from the challenge of simple arithmetic to the solution of an equation charting the orbit of a distant star. Each of the specialized sciences and the observations of friends and enemies provide a vocabulary and theory to label and explain diverse situations. We are concerned here, however, only with the situational aspects of hesitation and therefore with the ways in which principals judge and react to situations and in which observers observe those reactions.

It may be too facile to postulate extreme situations ranging from little to copious hesitation. As previously suggested, it is possible to proclaim that an exceptionally loud blast is heard by everyone, yet we immediately know also that the principal must be within the range of the sound, he must not be deaf, and perhaps he must be not so preoccupied with his own problems that the noise escapes his notice. A native speaker of English must pause when suddenly confronted with a sentence in Sanskrit, but not if he is a Sanskrit scholar. The situation created by the sudden and unexpected death of someone you know causes you to reflect before you can explain the tragedy by a reference to determinism or fate-destiny. Personality factors are unavoidable in every situation and therefore the guiding principle must be the truism that both judgments and actions result from an interaction of personality and situation, each of which can be weighted from close to zero to almost 99 percent as a result of the particular personality or situation at hand.

Interactions

Since interactions are complicated and messy, efforts are constantly made to consider one of these factors without the other. Observers are likely, for example, to ascribe situations as explanations for a principal's actions when they believe that most persons behave similarly in those situations or that a particular person repeatedly reacts similarly in a designated situation.[2] We have here a rough guide, but exceptions are too numerous. An extreme illustration: cases have been reported in which patients suffering from brain damage were unable to control their own violent behavior even though they may have sought to do so or have felt contrite for not having done so.[3] Here an organic factor produced a consistent deviation from "normal" behavior in a variety of situations usually requiring greater hesitation. A less exotic illustration can be lifted from any competitive sport. In baseball the person at bat can hesitate only a brief second as the pitched ball comes within striking range, yet it is self-evident that some players are more skillful than others in reaching the quick decision whether they should try to hit the ball and, if not, whether the umpire may call it a strike or a ball. The relation of personality to situations is one of the problems clinging to theorists and others since ancient times and hence it is perpetually and currently discussed and investigated by serious social scientists,[4] whether or not the question is considered "essentially meaningless" because both depend on the principal's "previous experience."[5]

The interaction between situation and principal is impressively demonstrated in the Matching Test. Here the situation is so constructed that some uncertainty is inevitable: it is highly unlikely that any subject, child or adult, has ever been confronted with a half dozen almost identical teddy bears, only one of which is exactly like the standard at the top of the sheet. The uncertainty, therefore, is situational at the outset, but quickly becomes internal and personal. As a result of the situation the principal hesitates, he is uncertain which judgment to make, eventually—if he continues to cooperate with the investigator—he passes judgment with or without being certain of his choice. Among animals, according to a group of British psychologists, "very general traits of persistence can be developed . . . by training them on schedules in which appetitive and aversive events are *unpredictably* intermingled";[6] the critical word here is "unpredictably," for then the subjects are uncertain whether they will be rewarded or punished and, presumably while hesitating, they continue to be motivated.

Inasmuch as an interaction between situation and personality is almost always inevitable, the only fruitful approach to relate these two variables to hesitation is to invoke a doctrine of probability: the degree of hesitation is likely to be less rather than greater when either variable is extremely important or compelling. For personality, for example, it is clear that most persons hear a loud noise, most non-Sanskrit scholars are puzzled by Sanskrit, many brain-damaged patients are impulsive, a famous baseball player hits the ball approximately four times out of ten. In such situations there is little hesitation since personality factors are salient. Similarly situations that are culturally saturated require little or no hesitation. When another person asks you for a glass of water, "you need not ask why he wants it."[7] Almost always in any situation you may assume without hesitation that he is not going to hurl the water in your face. But of course you have to understand English if that is the language in which the request has been made. For individual principals cultural determination resembles any consistently reinforced habit. You know your way around that town because you have been there many times, you need not hesitate and reflect to find your way about: you may not recall the names of the streets or be able to map the route you will follow, yet you almost instantly recognize where you are and where and how you must go.

As blatantly intimated in chapter 3, however, personality factors are seldom squeezed out of the judgments and behaviors of principals or explanations of observers. A touching incident, if true, is reported from Bali during the middle of the last century. A rajah had died and the culture of his society demanded that his corpse, being impure, be burned. A crucial part of the ceremony included the suttee: three of his concubines, "guiltless of any crime," also were to be consumed by the flames. When the fire began blazing, "the supreme moment" had arrived. Up to then the three women "showed no fear, still their chief care seemed to be the adornment of the body, as though making ready for life rather than death":

With firm and measured steps the victims trod the fatal plank; three times they brought their hands together over their heads, on each of which a small dove was placed, and then, with body erect, they leaped into the flaming sea below, while the doves flew up, symbolizing the escaping spirits.

Two of the women showed, even at the very last, no sign of fear; they looked at each other, to see whether both were prepared, and then, without stopping, took the plunge. The third appeared to hesitate, and to take the leap with less resolution; she faltered for a

moment, and then followed, all three disappearing without utter-
ing a sound.[8]

The heavily cultured situation triumphed over all three
women, but the personality of the one who hesitated in-
truded just a wee bit. And yet—somehow had the cultural
experience of that one been somewhat dissimilar from the
others, why was her personality perceptibly different?

Personality factors become more important when situations provide information that contradicts pre-existing stereotypes. In American society prejudices affect the way in
which the performance of tasks associated with gender is
evaluated and the actual performance itself. What happens
when females perform well in a position associated with males
(e.g., computer programming) or males in one usually allocated to females (e.g., nursing)?[9] The reply to the question
may be of no overpowering significance, but merely raising
the question demands hesitation: the very situation is not
governed by a cultural stereotype.

Weighting

Ideally it would be desirable to have some overall measure
that would weight the contribution of personality and situation (including other persons) to judgments and behavior
related to hesitation. In fact we have attempts to do just that;
but the calculations are based on studies in experimental situations and are difficult to generalize to more realistic situations.[10] Hesitation can vary from impulsivity to reflection
when principals are confronted with changes in their society
(Route 1b). Perhaps it is true, as has been argued, that living
organisms all have "an innate tendency to acquire knowledge" which "facilitates a flexible adaptation . . . to changing environmental conditions";[11] but surely "adaptation" requires careful definition. Crises arise and those affected panic:
they cry for help, they retreat without a plan, they sell their
stocks, or they attack those attacking them although in calmer
moments they would know they could not succeed. In unusual environments, such as those confronting men in Ant-

arctica, underwater exploration, and outer space, the reported accounts of principals indicate that they may
eventually experience some intellectual impairment, motivational decline, somatic complaints, and mood changes,[12]
as a consequence of which they probably hesitate, reflect,
and make adjustments in order to try to carry on their mis-
sions effectively. Judgments in changing situations such as
these stem in large part from the psychological equipment
which the principals bring to them. They are likely to cling
to whatever components have positive affective value for
them, for thus they can hope to repeat past rewards or at
least be attentive to such symbols.[13] Possibly, too, their com-
fort or discomfort in the new situation depends upon their
tendency to tolerate or not to tolerate ambiguity. Have they
a "dichotomizing attitude" that induces them to agree with
statements such as: "People can be divided into two distinct
classes: the weak and the strong" or "There is only one right
way to do anything"? If they do, it has been argued that they
would also agree somewhat with prophecies of: "Some day
a flood or earthquake will destroy everybody in the whole
world" and disagree with optimistic glimmers, "If everything would change, the world would be much better."[14] Or
then they are able to respond to a question of interest to
economists: "An individual is imagined to choose a plan of
consumption for a future time so as to maximize the utility
of the plan as evaluated at the present moment. . . . If he is
free to reconsider his plan at later dates, will he abide by it
or disobey it—even though his original expectations of future desires and means of consumption are verified?"[15]

In some situations the interaction of cultural or societal
and personality factors is so intricate that it is impossible to
assign more weight to one factor than to the other. Consider
the way in which principals cope with a temporal factor involving a delay in achieving their goal. Do they impulsively
select the immediate reward or do they hesitate and then
opt for the later one? In one experiment young American
children were shown an attractively wrapped gift but told
they could not open it until they completed a puzzle; in another experiment the children were offered the choice of re-

ceiving a less-preferred snack immediately or a more preferred one later. At first or second glance it might appear
that the two situations were similar since delay was the same
dependent variable being studied. Also in both studies the
children's personalities were assessed by their parents. In the
first study those children tolerating delay tended to be characterized as being "planful, thinks ahead" and *not* being
"unable to delay gratification." In the second study those who
delayed were thought to have "high standards for self" but
not to have high "intellectual capacity." Thus in the first situation the ability to delay was related consistently to positive attributes, but in the second to the absence of another
positive attribute, namely, that of so-called intellectual capacity.[16] If it can be assumed that the children and their parents in the two studies were similar—possibly a reckless,
though reasonable assumption—then it would seem that the
two situations were not similar, though both required delay,
and hence each drew upon different personality dispositions.
In addition, even the precise mode of presenting a delayed
reward may affect reactions. Thus preschool children, who
were compelled to wait before being given the opportunity
to play with toys they had been shown, tended to view the
real objects longer and hence presumably preferred them
more than they did a picture of them during the delay;[17]
presumably the real object was a more attractive substitute
for the pending reward than the symbolic substitute.

More generally, this need to choose between a present and
a future action requires some reflection, especially when one
of the alternatives is at a clearly perceived temporal distance from the moment of choice.[18] Should you visit a dentist now or later? If now, the pain will occur during the
pending visit, but the ordeal may avoid more compelling pain
later on; if later, there may be no pain now, but more pain
later. Should you refuse another alcoholic drink now and thus
deprive yourself of immediate pleasure, or accept it and then
perhaps suffer the penalty of a hangover or inappropriate
behavior? Will principals prefer the bird in the hand right
now or hope to obtain later two of the birds frolicking in the
bush? They may hesitate to reach a decision, although the

impulse may be to select the immediate reward; if the choice goes to the larger reward in the future, then the delay may signify an ability not to be impulsive but to await the future. Possibly adults planning investments may hesitate as they consider not only the length of the delay but also the magnitude of the reward and the probability of attaining it.[19] For children the reflection and the decision to receive the more distant reward may be related to conventionally measured intelligence and age, as suggested by a study—no, not this time conventionally among Americans—among deprived Arab refugee children in Jordan.[20]

Platitude or not, the degree of hesitation must depend upon how principals perceive the situation confronting them. The truism that the whole is often more than the sum of its parts is patently applicable to the groups in various situations. For when principals interact in a group, they create an atmosphere, a social climate, an ambience which may or may not be easily or immediately grasped either by themselves or by potential participants. For this reason principals often reflect before joining groups, and observers may find it difficult to predict or retrodict what did or will occur. Again, the details are needed.

In slightly different words, therefore, a situation, any situation, in the present or the past, close-by or in a distant land, is of interest and of significance to principals and observers only when it functions as a source of stimulation and only when and if aspects of it are somehow called to their attention. You may not know what happened in your community a generation ago, but those events are important to you perhaps because they have contributed to the strains and joys of your present everyday existence; you perceive some aspect of them. The misfortunes of your ancestors you yourself may have not experienced, yet you may be indignant when you hear about them and you may not hesitate to discriminate against persons in your society whose ancestors in turn committed the foul deeds. Yes, culture traits are bequeathed from one generation to the next, but they are inherited differently by principals whose degrees of hesitation concerning their mandated rules and duties vary.

Generally, therefore, past situations are remembered quite differently, depending upon the promptings that produce their recognition or recall. Probably many principals impulsively reply to banal questions concerning their residence, such as "How satisfied are you with X as a place to live?" and "How satisfied are you with the quality of life in X?" But when 800 citizens of Muncie, Indiana, the city once disguised as Middletown in a justly famous research project, were asked those questions and were also provided with a questionnaire containing statements to rate, they were able to pause and indicate whether they believed their community was beautiful to behold, had adequate educational facilities, permitted its citizens to share in making political decisions, and enabled new residents to become oriented there.[21] Some of their responses may have been spontaneous, but others were elicited by the questionnaire that induced them to reflect. When reflection with reference to such issues occurs, it is not surprising that individual or social differences appear. Persons in a British and in an American community responding to a comparable questionnaire concerning satisfaction with their places of residence revealed similar appraisals ("I feel very much that I belong here") as well as dissimilar ones ("This community is very peaceful and orderly").[22] Which sample, the British or the American, do you think tended to agree with the last statement about peace and orderliness and which of the two reflected longer to express their view?

The degree of hesitation may also be affected by the principal's anticipation either prior to or within a situation. You know what to expect, more or less, when you meet a group of friends. After you meet them, your initial impressions suggest whether on this particular occasion you will be bored or stimulated, vindicated or surprised. In a methodologically conventional situation subjects were once shown briefly exposed stimuli and asked to report what they had perceived. Their responses were influenced by a preparatory set given by the investigator; or they impulsively believed they perceived real words when, in fact, they had seen only skeleton words such as "pasrort."[23]

Finally, ambiguous situations provide insufficient knowledge which must be supplemented by more complete information. What happens when American motorists find themselves in the situation in which the car ahead fails to move forward when the traffic light turns from red to green? Certainly, with great acumen, we can predict that they quickly feel impatient; their impatience we know comes from the unnecessary delay in the situation. But do they honk their horns to inform the driver ahead that the signal has changed; if they do, how many seconds of reflection does it take them to do so? Both the response of honking by a sample of American drivers and its latency were once shown to depend not only on the length of the delay after the traffic light had turned from red to green but also on the momentary state of the drivers which had been induced while the light was still red by seeing female pedestrians (actually confederates of the investigator) who had been acting like clowns, who looked mildly sexually provocative, or who appeared to be quarrelling with each other.[24] Hesitation in this contrived but realistic situation thus depended on the objective delay and the driver's momentary mental state.

By now the pessimistic note being sounded in this chapter must be loud and opaque: it is almost always both dangerous and inaccurate to ascribe degrees of hesitation exclusively either to the situation or the personality, particularly when the individual principal has had an idiosyncratic background. The usually inevitable interaction between the two is applicable even to such an innocent subject as optimism. One treatise on that subject, though literary in style, contains frequent references to scholarly analyses and research. Its author calls optimism "as necessary as air" (the title of his first chapter): "making optimistic symbols and anticipating optimistic outcomes of undecided situations is as much part of human nature, of the human biology, as are the shape of the body, the growth of children, and the zest of sexual pleasure."[25] If optimism were really that necessary, it would be reasonable to expect such a cosmic view to appear frequently with little hesitation. In a conventional experiment, however, it was once demonstrated that the young Americans could be categorized as optimistic strategists or defensive pessimists. The optimists in this instance had high expectations for themselves before beginning a task and restructured their views when the outcome was known by ascribing successes to themselves and rationalizing failures; the pessimists had low expectations at the outset and hence prevented a loss of self-esteem. Before the experiment the principals had been categorized on the basis of their responses to a questionnaire (e.g., "I often think about what it will be like if I do very poorly in an academic situation"; "I generally go into academic situations with positive expectations about what I will do").[26] Here as in other studies there was a tendency for optimists, in comparison with pessimists, to be more successful in treating their own alcoholism, not to suffer postpartum depression,[27] to cope with stress,[28] and so on—and on and on. In these and other studies the principals selected the optimistic or pessimistic alternative on each of the items composing the questionnaire and, in addition, the sum of their scores on all the items fluctuated between extremes, with many or most scoring toward the middle of the scale. We might assume that those with extreme views hesitated less in passing judgment about events or in anticipating or rationalizing them and that those in-between hesitated more; yet the argument can be reversed by assuming that not less but more reflection is required to fit an event or an expectation into a pre-existing optimistic or pessimistic viewpoint.

Another kind of generalization has been expressed by a historian who argues that "the world's mood towards human progress" shifted from one of pessimism after World War I to one of hope and an "optimistic stance" immediately after World War II.[29] If this provocative, undocumented, undocumentable assertion be true, the "mood" for principals in the "world" must have been affecting the hesitation required to react emotionally to unspecified situations, but the guide here is quite risky. In many situations judgments and actions stem not from some overall feeling of optimism or pessimism but from other factors in the person-

alities and the situations. The historian's all-or-none or even
almost-all-or-almost-none assertion again, if true, is limited
but at least calls attention to cultural trends in situations.

Leadership

Some leaders lead and others follow their constituents—
by and large, every leader must do both and in varying combinations. That somewhat platitudinous, evasive statement
offers a challenge: to what degree does a leader hesitate as
the situations confronting him in his position require or enable him to make decisions concerning his followers? Does
he pursue his own goals; how does he take their goals into
account?

Evidence concerning the details of real-life decision-mak-
ing by those in power is hard to come by. Researchers do
not or cannot observe the actual processes, recorded tapes
are seldom available, and the officials themselves do not
necessarily report the complete truth to their subordinates
or the mass media. They may also deceive themselves. At the
time or later in their memoirs they probably offer necessarily incomplete or somewhat biased reports concerning themselves and events. Every tidbit must be carefully evaluated
and perhaps discounted. According to his testimony, President Truman never succumbed to hesitation: "A President
either is constantly on top of events or, if he hesitates, events
will soon be on top of him. I never felt that I could let up for
a single moment." And: "Once a decision was made, I did
not worry about it afterward."[30] Reinterpretation is necessary. Obviously, Mr. Truman hesitated before making certain decisions; for example, he consulted his cabinet and other
advisers. He could have meant that his hesitation was not
prolonged or that, after making a decision, he did not reflect
or have misgivings. In making these statements he may have
been seeking to strengthen his reputation as a strong character: according to some conventional wisdom, hesitation
signifies weakness.

Probably planning and issuing orders are less frequent or
innovative in the lower than in the upper echelons within

the structural hierarchy of a large organization. Perhaps, then, reflection accompanies increased responsibility. A moral warning must be issued: *Crimes of obedience*, the splendid and provocative title of a book,[31] are committed when principals commit deeds upon orders, whether or not they recognize the evil consequences. "What could I do, I was only a little man?", Adolf Eichmann stated as he explained why under orders from superiors he murdered thousands of Jews and Christians during World War II. People like Eichmann are too numerous to list but certainly also include other Germans who killed 300 Italians in caves outside Rome in 1944; Kurt Waldheim, the Austrian president, whose claim resembled Eichmann's after his role in sending Nazi prisoners to their doom was uncovered; participants in the Watergate scandal during the Nixon administration and the Iran-Contra blink-blank under Reagan—and so on, you have your own list. These individuals rest their evil case on one Critical Question, rule and duty, though we must suspect that the personality question also accounted for their behavior; but our judgment must be that their judgments that did not or could not include other Critical Questions were morally inadequate and must and should be condemned.

It is, perhaps, too easy to assume that decisions of leaders are reached after lengthy and profound hesitation because those decisions have far-flung effects upon their followers. Are they perforce in situations in which they must reflect concerning whether they should succumb to immediate pressures or consider the far-flung implications of what they decide? If oil is scarce and expensive, it is tempting to cut down trees on public lands in order to obtain fuel. But forests are important not only for the wood they provide but also for animals and the ecological system. Should the forests be sacrificed for the oil? Reflective perspective is essential. Much may depend upon who the decision-makers are: persons living near the forests have a viewpoint different from the lumber companies or from policy makers in distant parts.

The degree to which government leaders and diplomats hesitate before passing judgment, it may be somewhat easily assumed, depends initially upon their own style: some reflect at great length, others delay only briefly; some consult a large number of advisers, others weight the factors within themselves. A banal but critical issue is whether leaders really lead by following their own views or whether in fact they consult or are affected by the views of their followers. Their hesitancy depends, then, upon their own predispositions and the extent to which those tendencies are salient as well as upon situational factors requiring immediate actions or permitting delay. For better or worse, ever since the days of President Monroe and his doctrine, American presidents in a variety of situations have not hesitated regarding the policy to be invoked with reference to Latin American countries in which the United States is said to have "a special economic and security interest." Hesitation has usually been prolonged, however, concerning the implementation of that policy: should the Marines be sent in to block a potential invader, to overthrow a leader allegedly hostile to those American interests?[32] Leaders may also reflect less when they use "historical analogues" as policy guides. Colonel House, one of President Woodrow Wilson's advisers, reported that at the outset of World War I the president worried about the possibility of war with Great Britain since the British prior to the War of 1812 during the presidency of James Madison had also been illegally searching American ships. In addition, Madison had been "the only other Princeton [University] alumnus" besides himself to have been president.[33] Similarly President Truman, contrary to his assertion a few pages ago, is reported to have said, "I had trained myself to look back in history for precedents" as he later reviewed his decisions in office, especially with regard to the Korean war. And the policies of President Johnson and his advisers with respect to Vietnam are reported to have been influenced by the "alleged lessons" they believed they had learned from events in the 1930s.[34] When the "conceptual complexity" of the writings and speeches of prominent revolutionaries is carefully analyzed, it seems that the thinking of men who were successful in the post-revolutionary period (such as Jefferson and Lenin) was more complicated (that is, less polarized and more qualified or integrative) than those who were subsequent failures (such as, Hamilton or Trotsky).[35] Possibly, after the battle was won, those remaining in power were able to reflect more carefully than those who were ousted.

The decisions of those in power are also affected by pressure groups and by the expressions of constituents often referred to vaguely as public opinion. Probably, conventional wisdom again suggests, these influences are of greater significance in democratic than in so-called authoritarian regimes. An illustration suggests how the appeasement theme just mentioned has been employed in the United States. Before the Senate considered ratifying the Gorbachev-Reagan intermediate-range nuclear forces (INF) treaty of 1987, and to prevent further agreements between the two countries, the Conservative Caucus of Republicans, among other appeals, published an advertisement with a picture of Chamberlain and Hitler directly above those of Reagan and Gorbachev under the headline, "Appeasement is Unwise in 1988 as in 1938".[36] To what extent do leaders reflect upon the validity or relevance of such claims? It has been said that a main function of diplomacy in fact is to affect what has often been called the images of an opponent so that the leaders of the opposing government hesitate to take certain action and hence eventually react or do not react in the desired manner.[37]

Delay, reflect creatively, in order to acquire relevant information and advice. Postponement, if not procrastination, may well be the better part of wisdom.

Reflection, however, does not guarantee morally sound judgments. Some form of graft or corruption appears to exist in almost all non-traditional societies, whether they lean toward acclaimed democracy, socialism, or communism. The explanation for their origin and existence in some principals need not deter us, for we would note only that the tendency to succumb to temptation, not to hesitate forever to do so, increases in the presence of models which then make the crimes appear safe and almost respectable.

There may be little or no relation between the viewpoint of leaders, political or otherwise, and their audience's hesitancy or acceptance of what is communicated. In Western societies the mass media provide their audiences with pseudo-

situations consisting of large doses of information and view-
points that may or may not be in accord with people's pre-
conceptions. While it may be true that they report only the
highlights of events, the headlines or a summary lasting only
a few seconds,[38] the audience then may either accept or reject what they have seen or heard with little or no reflection;
or else the snippet inspires them to contemplate the implication for or the relevance to themselves. Through those media, moreover, information may be unwittingly acquired that
has consequences for future hesitation. During the 1980s in
the United States it was widely reported that some persons
had pushed razor blades into apples, and other edible food
that subsequently were given to young children as they went
"begging" during the ritual of Halloween. Such sadistic acts,
an investigation revealed, were "greatly exaggerated."[39] Many
parents, however, impulsively believed the incident to be
widespread and hence sensibly hesitated and then prevented
their children from accepting or eating such gifts.

The most dismal failure of leaders occurs when followers
revolt and therefore threaten or overthrow the existing re-
gime. A political scientist who has examined various modern
rebellions concludes that the background for violence is "a
diffuse disposition toward aggressive action" in addition to
what the followers perceive to be a discrepancy between "their
present existence and what they believe is their due."[40] After
the Chinese students' uprising in the late spring of 1989, he
might well have added non-violent protest. Such general
preparation presumably strengthens the impulse to become,
join, or support the rebels, to throw stones or bombs, or to
sacrifice oneself.

> *IN SHORT: after the theoretical hesitancies of previous chapters,
> it is essential to proclaim an ultimate challenge which is to
> evaluate the situational constraints and opportunities confronting
> principals, whatever their culture, society, personalities, and the
> persons or groups influencing them; the ensuing process of
> weighting concerns both principals, especially leaders making
> decisions, and observers like the rest of us.*

7

Desirability and Value

At this point an abrupt, perhaps welcome change is made away from explaining why, how, and when principals experience degrees of hesitation. Instead, attention is focused upon the desirability of being relatively impulsive or reflective: at a given moment or over time why should the principal incline in one direction rather than in the other? Yes, the key word is *should*, the challenge is a moral one.

In chapter 4 some of the research has been reviewed that would determine whether young children tend to be impulsive or reflective by noting how quickly and how accurately they respond to predetermined, arbitrary situations such as the Matching Test: tell me, dear subject, which one of these six teddy bears is exactly like the teddy bear at the top of the two rows of bears. In all or at least in almost all instances, children termed reflective on the basis of their performances on such a test tended to be "superior" in other situations, and their superior performance is thought to be desirable in Western society. It is considered good, for example, to be able to recall past experiences accurately, to comprehend easily what one reads, to reason precisely, and so on. Probably children grow more reflective, however measured, with increasing age, which means that both they and their socializing agents come to value that mode of judging and acting. At least in this ethnocentric sense, therefore, reflection is preferred. But is such praise only ethnocentric? Perhaps not: greater economy is usually sought in any society, no matter what task is being performed. Self-control regarding bodily functions and good behavior, as maintained in chapter 3, is presumably encouraged everywhere. Extreme impulsivity can also be deplored on psychiatric grounds when it is associated with dyslexia, gambling, kleptomania, pyromania, hyperactive children, other early "conduct disorders," and "sociopathic tendencies, especially when anxiety is low."[1]

Almost without exception studies of hesitation that reveal the investigator's value judgment assume or declare that impulsivity is to be condemned. In the appendix to this book listing actions associated with impulsivity, very, very few studies praise such actions (section 6). Yes, there are exceptions, such as the one mentioned in chapter 3 concerning the very low, unimpressive relation among German students between two standardized measures of impulsivity and "planfulness."[2] In contrast is a longish list of undesirable behavior associated with impulsivity (section 3); alphabetically it begins with abnormality and ends with unstable personal or social relations. In the same appendix the list of ensuing handicaps extends from borderline psychopathologies to schizophrenia (section 4); and yet another list refers to disorders associated with psychological processes ranging from attention to verbalization (section 5).[3] The flavor of these characterizations is evident in the following description of "high impulsivity" that is said to be one of the three major features of psychopathology:

The psychopath cannot wait. He must have his pleasure now and cannot abide delay. His time sense is disturbed, and he cannot work toward distant goals. He is at the mercy of his impulses and is susceptible to momentary temptation or escape from aversiveness, regardless of later negative consequences.[4]

Halt, may one skeptically ask what is bad about any of these attributes? Why not follow the guide of *carpe diem* and seize the moment or the day here and now? Is reference being made only to a syndrome of impulsive actions and not to the isolated impulse that produces poetry or the avoidance of imminent danger? The American students whose paper-and-pencil responses once suggested that they experienced difficulties as they sought to cope with problems were found also to be persons "who harbor resentments, are suspicious, irritable, guilty and who prefer to express their hostility in individual ways,"[5] certainly ingredients which require self-defeating reflection. Ah me, let us momentarily forget the impulsive interruption and carry on in the hallowed tradition that praises reflection. Both common experience concerning the difficulties encountered when obese persons seek to diet or alcoholics to curb their drinking proclivities as well as experimental and empirical studies on delays of present gratifications for the sake of greater rewards in the future, moreover, also suggest that curbing impulses is either necessary or desirable.[6] Otherwise, the individual steals the snack, has just one more drink, or forgets for the moment the future value of a momentary sacrifice. Possibly, as once demonstrated in Israel, delinquents have a more restricted future time perspective and tend to estimate that brief temporal intervals are shorter than comparable nondelinquents;[7] they may be less able to provide themselves with the opportunity to reflect concerning long-range plans or to be less impulsive concerning the passing of time. A plague on impulsivity.

Sometimes psychologists in the West have considered that judgments concerning the actions of other persons, real or imaginary, are less egocentric and hence morally superior when they refer not to a Critical Question regarding the consequences of those actions but to the intentions of the principals. Premeditated murder is judged more severely than the "accidental" slaying of another person. Canadian children around the ages of four and seven were once asked to judge why characters in a brief film or story were "naughty." Those classified as impulsive as rated by their teachers or by

their performance on the Matching Test or a simpler equivalent for the younger children tended to select the allegedly
inferior moral standard of consequences rather than intentions.[8]

Typical of the influential praise showered upon reflection
are the fables of the fabled Aesop who presumably lived,
possibly as a slave, in Greece during the sixth century B.C. A
close if subjective reading has failed to uncover a single tale
documenting the view that he who hesitates is lost. A woman,
unable to reform her alcoholic husband, places him while
drunk in a tomb; upon awakening he believes himself in the
land of the dead and still wants "a little drink, I beseech
thee"; she thus learns that "drunkenness is an incurable habit"
that cannot be impulsively altered. Aesop, therefore, en-
thrones reflection and patience. When the Sow and the Bitch
debate concerning their fecundity, the Sow agrees that the
Bitch "brought more in a litter, and oftener, than any other
four-legged creatures . . . but you are always in so much
haste about it that you bring Puppies into the world blind."
In his edition of Aesop, an eighteenth century archdeacon
adds a postscript to each story in which, at greater length
than the fables themselves, he provides an ethnocentric explanation and often an illustration of each story. The most
cited fable, perhaps, of the fox calling the grapes he could
not reach "green and sour," that theologian converted into
the human realm with the following gem: "A young fellow
being asked how he liked a celebrated beauty, by whom all
the world knew he was despised, answered, she had a stink-
ing breath."[9] Both Aesop and the clergyman thus condemn
the "pride" and inadequate hesitation that facilitate rationalization, yet the fox and the lad at least found some consolation in their frustrated state.

Aesop and the archdeacon concentrate upon individual
principals, but selecting a degree of hesitation becomes a bit
more complicated when groups of persons hesitate. Almost
never, for example, does a large body like the U.S. Congress
reach a decision quickly. Conflicting interests have to be re-
solved not only among members of the House of Represen-
tatives and the Senate, but also between those two legisla-

tive bodies. In addition, information and pressure come from constituents, lobbyists, other government agencies, and sometimes from experts of all sorts. Is such hesitation good or bad? No overall judgment can be rendered, too many factors are involved. If the proposed legislation is urgent—no matter how urgency is defined, a value judgment must be passed—the delay might be condemned politically or morally. If an environmental issue is being discussed before a committee, such as one involving the control of a pesticide or the preservation of land for a wilderness area or a national park, the evaluation of the delay depends upon the evaluation of the outcome which may be "good" or "bad." Each legislator of course also hesitates and is affected by what transpires during hearings and congressional debates.

Indeed, more generally, to hesitate briefly or at length, to reflect or not to reflect are questions of supreme universal and moral importance. Clearly, the choice depends in large part on the goal to be achieved: what will I do? But other aspects of morality may also be involved. To what extent do they, whoever they are, permit me to hesitate: what may I do, what must I do? To ask these Critical Questions and then to seek answers to them is based on the bold assumption that principals are able to decide how long they will hesitate and whether they should reflect. Why bold?

Bold, because in many circles the assertion is thus made that principals have the freedom to intervene by coming to a decision of their own selection. When a course of action or a degree of hesitation is desirable, it is presumed that principals may be able within limits to select the more or most promising one. Determinists are quick to deny and refute such a bold assumption, for they believe quite righteously that if—if, if, if—a competent observer has all the relevant facts, he can anticipate or predict what the choice would be and hence the choice is predetermined and the principal is not free to choose.

Perhaps the deterministic critic is correct, at least in theory: freedom does not exist, intervention is a subjective illusion. But, some, maybe many, even most, principals believe, whether deluded or not, that they have been free and are now free to hesitate in varying degrees. What do you do, I ask again, when you are offered the choice of meat or fish, of wine or whiskey? You may hesitate more than a millisecond and then you know or you believe you know that it is you, your self, who makes the choice. What style of clothes will you buy? Where are you going on vacation next year? When you die, do you want your body to be buried below or above ground, do you favor cremation? From your standpoint, from what goes on within you as you answer questions more or less subtle than these, you know what you are thinking or feeling as you hesitate, and it is you who make the choice. You and the determinists really part company only slightly when faced with these questions: as observers they try to explain what you are experiencing; certainly as the principal you believe the experience of hesitating is real, whether they call your freedom to choose an illusion which they puncture deterministically or whether they refer to your fate-destiny (variable linkage). You are quite aware that you desire fish rather than meat because you have enjoyed no fish for about two weeks, that you are in the mood for wine rather than whiskey, that you prefer clothes that are not too conspicuous, that you will spend your next vacation at a place you once liked tremendously years back, and that you oppose cremation for reasons you are reluctant to mention. If an omniscient or perspicacious observer predicts beforehand how you will respond to such questions, well and good, provided his prediction helps rather than hinders you; but it is you who hesitates to some degree, and it is you who supplies the answers to yourself or to any observer asking you to reply.

At the very least the determinist must concede that a belief in freedom is part of a collection of many beliefs affecting decisions and actions, and therefore it is absolutely essential to include that belief in the deterministic bundle. "If men define situations as real, they are real in their consequences"[10]—but which consequences; all consequences? Impulsivity and reflection have no virtue as such: the specific consequences that result from the decision to intervene or from the action are to be evaluated. When principals are confronted with problems for which no immediate solutions seem evident, they do hesitate: they seek new information, evaluate old information, and weigh possible alternatives. While thus hesitating, their modes of thinking are likely to be most varied. Even a very specialized group, presumably Americans concerned with business administration, it has once been suggested, resorted to five different "sets of strategies" during periods of hesitation and cogitation. Fancy and intriguing names have been plastered upon persons employing the modes: synthesist, idealist, pragmatist, analyst, and realist. In addition, a particular American may indicate that he or she employs a combination of these types.[11]

The most valiant or determined believer in freedom must thus agree that freedom is not unlimited, unless he interprets reflexes such as sneezing, vomiting, and pulling back one's hand from a hot or sharp object as actions that free the individual "from harmful contacts" which "almost all living things" do.[12] Part of the subjective, cognitive belief in freedom includes an awareness of the limitations. In this chapter, therefore, it is necessary to consider the no-choice condition in which through necessity the principal realizes that he is unable to exercise free choice completely. Then we can turn to situations in which he believes he has freedom: what is it desirable for him to do? Unabashedly and without apology we transcend science and objectivity in order to concentrate upon morality: when and for what reasons is it desirable to hesitate to some degree?

"Ah, but a man's reach should exceed his grasp. / Or what's a heaven for?"[13] The somewhat hackneyed poetic truth of Robert Browning is echoed by a psychologist who indicates that even young children "frequently" prefer to achieve goals through their own efforts, rather than those easily attained. The aspiration, however, cannot exceed the grasp too far, for then frustration and failure may result. After failure, the individual may then seek a goal too far below or above his ability in order, respectively, to be certain of success or to compensate for his previous failure.[14] In any case, setting the level of aspiration requires some reflection and is desirable for the attainment of satisfaction. The precise amount of reflection cannot be specified because it depends on the nature of the goal to be attained as well as upon the principal's own experience and modes of thinking.

We need no poet to remind us that we often do not achieve the goals we seek, but then, in the midst of disappointment and frustration, what do we do? We hope, we hope to do better, to avoid past mistakes, to find people more sensible, or—whatever this means—to have our society improve. "Only when the person gives up hope does he stop 'actively reaching out': he loses his energy, he ceases planning, and, finally, he even stops wishing for a better life."[15] Hoping of this sort is not a reflex, though some principals may begin a fantasy almost instantly after defeat. Reflection concerning the present and future status is essential. Hesitation comes to the rescue.

Hesitation may facilitate or inhibit other human tendencies with which it is interrelated, or it may be a consequence of them. Suppose it is considered desirable to cultivate "optimism" because such a disposition may be closely related to the desirable value of coping.[16] One can argue that reflection is a byproduct of optimism or that being optimistic requires reflection before the brighter side of events or persons can be appreciated in a gloomy, competitive society. Hesitation, consequently, precedes or follows the realization of the accompanying dispositions that are considered praiseworthy. The artist Rodin is reported to have declared that "patience is also a form of action."[17] That thought provokes two interpretations. For the observer patience is action in the sense that delaying or doing "nothing" while being patient communicates a message or blocks faulty action that might otherwise have occurred. For the principal the action is being internalized: he must be engaging in mental trial-and-error, he must be inhibiting himself, he may be creative.

Also praised in Western society is fantasy. On the basis of experiments, unfortunately as ever largely with Americans, we think we know that fantasy, an activity that does not advance "some intrinsic goal extrinsic to the situation itself" and hence is not directly concerned with problem solving, may have various laudable functions. It may subsequently modify behavior; it may reflect "unresolved current problems, unfinished tasks, role conflicts, and prominent affective responses, as well as the challenges of identity and commitment posed by the individual's social relationships"; it may be a substitute for aggression that cannot be overtly expressed. Often, therefore, it is "indistinguishable" from planning.[18] We dare not, however, sing a hymn of uncritical praise to fantasy since such activity can defeat planning when it is a way of escaping from reality rather than being creative and plunging into appropriate action.

Related to fantasy is curiosity, the motivation for which may be most varied.[19] The principal is bored: for the moment or over time he has achieved his significant goals and therefore seeks to recapture the thrills and satisfaction of being successful. He is confronted with a changed or novel situation that requires exploration if he is not to be uncomfortable or frustrated. Or he himself deliberately creates the change that then requires him to search for a new solution. In any case he must hesitate and reflect which may be considered morally good.

No easy generalization is available that would indicate the factors associated with creativity in fields like science, literature, music, and leadership. There are statistical generalizations that indicate modal tendencies; possibly, for example, according to one study, "though a certain amount of formal education may enhance the probability of creative achievement, beyond a certain point additional training seems to decrease the chances of attaining eminence." Other background factors are associated with creativity, such as birth order, peers functioning as models, age, the Zeitgeist, and the principal's motivation.[20] But does the creative act itself, when it occurs, represent the culmination of a long period of reflection or an impulsive leap away from experience and convention? We do not know, yet we must suspect that some degree of hesitation may occur for some persons or in some situations (Routes 2b or 3b).

One area of human concern that stresses the desirability of reflection both practically and morally is that of religion.

In some faiths too much hesitation concerning the cosmic issues is discouraged, because the faithful may then desert the fold; yet simultaneously some reflection concerning the established truths may be encouraged, for thereby it is hoped that faith will be strengthened. Missionary religions deliberately seek to have the unconverted reflect regarding their present beliefs and practices as well as the efforts they make or fail to make concerning their own eternal earthly and heavenly hopes and problems: reflection, they think, may lead to a rejection of the old and a conversion to the new. At some so-called revival meetings in the United States, however, the clergyman may attempt to stir emotions so deeply that members of the congregation impulsively pledge their adherence to his denomination or sect as well as a financial contribution.

The rhapsodic praise of reflection and condemnation of impulsivity must again be interrupted. Sometimes impulsivity may be determined, as indicated in connection with the Matching Test in chapter 2, by considering only foreground factors (Routes 1a and 2a) without paying more than lipservice to other Routes. At the spur of the moment he agreed to participate in the robbery or she agreed to become sexually involved. Aside from failing to consider background factors that predispose the principal to be impulsive in that particular situation, the observer and maybe even the principal himself or herself fails to investigate those predispositions or perhaps events that have facilitated the so-called impulsive judgment or action. Morally, moreover, the person is thus damned without determining whether he or she is responsible in any sense for the proclivity leading to the judgment and action. Neither of our hypothetical persons, for example, may have been adequately socialized in terms of the norms we consider to be good.

Hesitation itself, whether good or bad, has a temporal attribute. For convenience and also because most of us do not usually think in terms of a continuum, the desirable durations are considered here under three arbitrary and artificial headings: "no" (little), some, and considerable. The "no" is embedded in quotation marks for an obvious reason that has been previously mentioned: the fastest human response to external stimulation requires some delay before the nervous system of the principal reacts.

"No" (Little) Hesitation

An event can be experienced either as an effect or as a cause. You avoid an oncoming car without thinking; afterwards you are frightened, you have not had the opportunity to hesitate very long before or during the event that clearly is the cause of your action. Or, you wonder whether to visit a particular person, in which case your hesitation affects or causes your behavior by delaying or accelerating it. Can you choose whether to hesitate deliberately or not and hence to select the significant link in the chain causing or not causing your decisions and actions?

Immediately we note situations in which principals are deprived of the freedom to hesitate, such as—once more— the blinking of the eye after stimulation by a bright light and the startle resulting from hearing a loud noise. Freedom is absent: we blink or cringe without reflection (Route 1a). Here the response is part of human equipment and may serve a biological function to protect the eye or to push the organism into a state of readiness. The value is that of survival by avoiding pain or destruction. No moral quibble here, although we can imagine conditions in which the principal learns or seeks to control the amplitude of the reflex response. As we know from looking at the facts, the state of the organism prior to stimulation affects minutely the speed of the reaction, so that in the limited metaphysical sense you can increase or decrease your hesitation by means of drugs, exercise, or any prior action that has impact upon the overall state of your organism. A moral decision here has limited value, yet can be significant when the principal wonders whether he should endure the rigors of training to become a first-class athlete or instead pay attention to other pursuits.

A minimum of hesitation is desirable when no hesitation seems feasible: the principal is commanded to conform to a request by a powerful person and to be threatened with punishment if he refuses. Can he then imagine a better solution than to conform? Here we must think of martyrs and heroic persons who endure physical torture and sometimes death rather than to recant, to reveal secrets, or to betray a trust. Impulsivity, "no" hesitation, thus is often both necessary and desirable. It is essential to avoid a passing danger when driving a car or walking close to a precipice on a mountain trail; it is desirable to live rather than to perish. An athlete in most sports must react quickly without reflecting if he or she is to win; and winning for a good or bad reason is believed to be desirable (Route 3a). These illustrations, one must immediately add, are quite obvious. More significant is carrying out the impulse to help another human being who is in distress or who simply requires assistance to enable him to achieve his goal or to achieve it more readily. Or when another person grieves, you do not or should not laugh but somehow offer sympathy or consolation. Empathy, which tends to be such a strong impulse that it has been included among the central dispositions discussed tentatively in chapter 4, does not guarantee moral perfection since the sympathetic person may share the feelings of someone engaging in an evil practice.

Impulsivity can lead to judgments and actions that are not only prejudiced in an evil sense but also to those that can be commended from another moral standpoint. We praise persons who are committed to a cause and who therefore reveal "consistent lines of activity"; and we also employ similar terminology somewhat loosely to suggest that whole societies are committed or are consistent.[21] If the objective is laudable, then so is the commitment or the consistency. The moral problem becomes a pedagogical one: how can persons be taught or be persuaded to become committed or remain consistent so that with little or "no" hesitation they reject deviation from principles they or even you and I consider morally good?

Spontaneity likewise involves little hesitation. The principal quickly reaches a decision or relies on a pre-existing disposition and immediately responds. He may wish to demonstrate to another person his trust, confidence, or lack of suspiciousness. To do something on the spur of the moment, as the phrase goes, is often praised in Western society, though the penalty or punishment therefrom may soon appear. What seems to an observer to be spontaneous, however, may have been more or less premeditated by the principal; or that observer may discount the apparent spontaneity of the action by explaining it through a reference to the principal's predispositions or background (variable linkage).

In some situations the principal has a role to perform and does not permit himself to hesitate in order to consider alternatives. An actor in a play must literally follow the script, even when on occasion as a person he may prefer another line or action different from that prescribed by the dramatist; yet he is able within limits to control the precise way in which he interprets many aspects of his role. A friend greets you and then, unless you wish to insult or slight him, you immediately respond by acknowledging his greeting and greet him in return, although of course your degree of cordiality varies.

We are asked a question and we reply as quickly as possible because we wish to demonstrate that we are not stupid, that we are willing and able to provide the information being sought. It is against our interest to hesitate very long and we know it. The ball, in whatever game we are playing, is coming our way and, though we may imagine it is beyond our reach, we do reach out and attempt to do what the situation demands. *Carpe diem* once more, the moment, the opportunity may not arise again or at least for some time. The winner in the lottery may gain millions, somebody is bound to win, a ticket must be bought within the hour because thereafter no more tickets will be sold.

Seizing the moment, however, may be difficult: the principal may not be certain that the day or the moment is the right one or he may not be able to anticipate whether or not the opportunity will arise again. Physical or moral courage may be required to plunge right now rather than to await another or better opportunity later on. Under almost all circumstances, particularly for the principal himself or his psychiatrist, a continued depression is to be avoided or alleviated. During such an episode the individual suffers from a "loss of interest or pleasure in all or almost all usual activities and pastimes."[22] Clearly the depressed person is not achieving the goals others and he himself in a non-depressed state would attain. Action is needed, not prolonged hesitation or reflection. But what action? The moral question is unavoidable.

The most extreme form of "irrational" impulsivity occurs among maniacs, such as persons who cannot refrain from stealing even though doing so is not necessary or against their own interests (kleptomania); possibly compulsive gamblers are in the same category.[23] Schizophrenics, on the other hand, hesitate maladaptively: they may hesitate in old situations when it is not necessary to do so or fail to hesitate when hesitation is necessary or desirable.[24] Both of the above portraits are oversimplified but would only suggest that hesitation can be one of the symptoms in serious disorders. Less complicated behavior can be culled from everyday existence. When presumably normal American college students, for example, were once asked whether they would be inclined—at least hypothetically—to gamble when their chances of winning were 5, 10, or 15 percent versus their chances of losing were 95, 90, or 85 percent, there was a slight tendency, especially among the males, to be more willing to gamble when the odds were phrased positively rather than negatively.[25] A moment of reflecting before leaping might have convinced the susceptible principals that they were being confronted only with different phrasings of identical probabilities.

Quickly, then, in summary: "no" or little hesitation is generally condemned, but the exceptions are both noteworthy and puzzling.

Some Hesitation

Evidence at hand suggests a relation, a negative one, between inability to hesitate and what might be called mental stability. Sixteen "hyperactive" American boys, for example, were once given the choice of solving either a small number of arithmetical problems to secure a few toys immediately or many more problems to obtain a larger number later on; they had been classified as hyperactive because they were known to be "inattentive, impulsive, and easily frustrated." In comparison with a comparable control group of non-hyperactive boys, they tended to prefer the immediate and smaller reward. Caution: there was no difference between the two groups when confronted with varying numbers of tasks to be completed and corresponding rewards to be obtained but with no delays.[26] More generally, many human accomplishments depend on the ability and inclination to forego immediate satisfaction for the sake of greater gratification in the future. Agriculturalists must wait until their plants mature before harvesting them; in any society surplus capital cannot be expended immediately if new enterprises are to be encouraged and flourish in the future. Some hesitation is essential before delays appear tolerable.

The ability to hesitate more than briefly is often useful and morally good when the delay enables the principal to acquire additional information related to more of the Critical Questions, to reply more completely, and thus to carry on satisfactorily. Herewith are typical examples of impulsive views that reflection conceivably could puncture:

I liked him from the start and nothing he ever did subsequently changed my opinion.

I am going to vote for him because he looks so attractive on television.

I think I shall buy it because a person I admire recommends it in a newspaper advertisement.

I am not worried about pollution or the ozone layer because the air around me seems pure.

He was a gifted person and did well until his luck ran out.

I believe it because all the people I know, without exception, believe it.

That cannot be right, I don't want to accept it.

To avoid such errors, probing and reflection are needed; at least some hesitation is essential. An administrator in an academic institution once declared, "I make decisions and I make them fast; nobody can criticize me for sitting on my tail." But we did criticize many of his decisions, speedy or slow, because they often stemmed from his prejudices and failure to reflect. Perhaps the cliché, "look before you leap," summarizes the wise dictum to follow, provided of course looking not only is possible but also results in better guides to productive behavior.

Even momentary, relatively slight hesitation, consequently, has many advantages. The principal is given the opportunity to recall relevant experience from the past, and thus to appreciate his successes or failures in the same or similar situations (Route 3b). Decades or so ago it was suggested that the "facilitative effect" of such knowledge is "one of the best established findings in the research literature"; thereby the individual has learned the types of error, if any, he has committed; in addition he may be motivated "to try harder and persist longer" in the future.[27] Stray bits of evidence suggest that deviant behavior may be related to impulsivity rather than reflection. The time span of the stories of non-delinquent boys in response to the investigator's request ("I'll tell you a story and then let you finish it any way you want to") was once longer than that of a comparable delinquent group.[28] Evidently, the delinquents sought to have events take place more rapidly than the controls, possibly because they failed to reflect concerning cultural regulations and penalties.

From the perspective of social evolution, one writer has speculated, hesitancy has had great utility: early hunters must have learned that the game they needed in order to survive would not be immediately available but had to be tracked down. Rather than feeling hopeless at the start of the hunt they must have reflected and planned their tactics on the basis of hunts in the past and the situation at hand. Likewise persons who believe they will benefit from over-the-counter drugs or from the superfluous vitamins they purchase reflect and hope their lot will improve; and perhaps their very hope facilitates the feeling of improvement.[29] Like the placebos distributed in some scientific experiments?

"To become accustomed to anything is a terrible thing," a Japanese Zen master once told a well-rounded anthropologist who himself argues persuasively for the value of what he calls "flexibility." That value he thinks must apply both to individuals and the societies in which they live. Otherwise the relation between them and their environment is disturbed and evils such as deforestation, famine, epidemics, and overpopulation ensue. The environment has certain inherent limitations that human beings must recognize if they are to survive or at least if some kind of evolutionary process is to continue. Such so-called biological needs also depend upon the interaction of many factors; thus "eating is governed by appetite, habit, and social convention rather than hunger"—that is, exclusively by hunger, he might well have added.[30] One must reflect, therefore, and realize the natural resources of the earth will be utilized differently only after the human agents themselves have learned new ways to survive.

Some hesitation may help to inhibit snap judgments ranging from those based on simple perception to those embodying personal or what is called conventional wisdom. A very provocative illustration is provided by the so-called Müller-Lyer illusion which has appeared in many psychology textbooks and which is reproduced below. The two lines are of equal length; yet, even knowing the truth, you continue to perceive one to be larger than the other—with very little hesitation. Reflection thus can be efficacious only when the principal has learned that sometimes even his own senses must be distrusted; he must be wary. The sun does not rise and set each day, however apparent its appearance and disappearance unequivocally seem to be.

Like the senses, folk wisdom is difficult to reject, especially when it is clothed in appealing shades of apparent veracity. There is said, for example, to be a human tendency to consider scarce commodities desirable or valuable simply because they are scarce and hence usually require greater outlays of effort or money. The reasons for their scarcity may be real (a work of art that is one of a kind) or artificial (a producer deliberately limits the supply of a commodity so

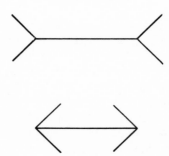

that few are available; or the price may be set so high that few can afford to purchase it). Before the principal makes a sacrifice to acquire the scarce commodity, he would do well to hesitate and discover how important it is for his designated needs thus to be satisfied. It is often necessary to distinguish between the valid and invalid components of a stereotype; thus in Western society the principal may be able to infer correctly the gender of an infant or a very small child from the color or type of clothing being worn but he must be wary concerning any additional inference concerning personality characteristics derived from assumed gender and allegedly related gender attributes.[31]

Political issues offer challenges that often remain unrecognized because of their complexity. Do you approve or disapprove of your country's foreign policy concerning unfriendly countries? Do you think it important that we be stern or conciliatory? Do you show concern for your security and therefore advocate an increase in military expenditures? Many persons may have strong attitudes on these subjects and hence, when queried, they may be able easily to offer their viewpoint. But have they considered the relation between foreign policy and economic factors such as foreign debts, balance of trade, the stability of the country's currency, and the day-by-day welfare of their fellow citizens? These economic matters may be crucial determinants of diplomatic decisions but may not be taken into account when political attitudes are expressed. Reflection is desirable.

Permit a personal experience. Since the Munich Pact of

September 1938 I have had a most unfavorable opinion of Neville Chamberlain, the British Prime Minister, who even after the Nazis had incorporated Austria into Germany, signed a pact with Hitler permitting the Germans to invade and incorporate Czechoslovakia's Sudetenland. Chamberlain's policy of appeasement I knew was wrong: it enabled Hitler that same year to seize the remainder of Czechoslovakia and then later it led to World War II and its horrors. Unhesitatingly I have been calling Chamberlain a weakling, an opinion strongly fortified by my own experiences: I had studied in Germany during the two years immediately before Hitler came to power and hence appreciated the ruthlessness of Nazidom; good German friends of mine had been killed by the Nazis; and in 1939 I became a government official concerned with American psychological warfare against Hitler and the enemies of the United States during that war. Furthermore, I have been strongly opposed to war in any form since the ending of World War II and hence have supported all steps leading to disarmament. Suddenly, on the fiftieth anniversary of the Munich Pact, I chanced to hear on the radio a realistic reenactment of the 1938 events, replete with the actual voices of Chamberlain, Churchill, Hitler, and commentators and reporters of that day.[32] Before and during Munich, contrary to my belief, Chamberlain had been "widely admired" at home and in Europe; Roosevelt praised him. I listened to Chamberlain movingly express his aversion to war based on his country's experience in World War I; another war, he said, would destroy European civilization. He insisted that peace through negotiation was more important than preventing Hitler, for the benefit of "a faraway country," from annexing the Sudetenland. Later in the same recapitulation I heard him admit that Munich and appeasement had been a mistake. That agreement, broken by Hitler six months later, the same broadcast reminded me, gave Britain a year to strengthen its military establishment which in 1938 had not been "in any shape to go to war." This replaying of an historical event made me reflect: had I been misjudging Chamberlain, had I been blindly and impulsively opposed to any concession to Hitler and in favor of agreements or treaties that ostensibly support peace but might lead to disaster; should the view prevail that negotiations are risky unless the negotiators are strong? The strange aspect of this radio experience is the fact that I had heard Chamberlain and the others back in 1939, that I had drawn my own conclusions, but that now I was unexpectedly required to hesitate and rethink my view of him and the ensuing events. Isn't it possible, I asked myself, and I ask you, to have a cherished belief that subsequent events or reinterpretations of past events may not explode? Must we ever reflect before believing anything even when we ourselves have experienced what we have come to believe?

Praise for some hesitation must always be tempered with a warning. Unless reflection occurs in the interval or unless events change, hesitation can become a form of procrastination: avoiding a difficult or unpleasant decision or a course of action in the hope that the mere passing of time will produce greater wisdom, more knowledge, or a more favorable situation. The principal's error is to imagine that delaying has virtues in its own right. In addition, pausing can enable one to rationalize and thus convert the displeasing into the pleasing, a judgment that may be either incorrect or morally wrong. Another way to escape reality, perhaps indulged in universally, is to utilize cultural traditions to peer into the past or the future, especially when the pressures of the moment are overwhelming. In Western tradition we look backward into the Garden of Eden or even into our own childhood "when life was simple and people were better in the good old days." Or a utopia is postulated: "Zion will become . . . a natural Eden."[33] He who hesitates thus finds gratifying compensations but again only by fleeing from the problem at hand. Once more the same skeptical note: some hesitation can be helpful, useful, or good; yet it is not a panacea.

Considerable Hesitation

Any systematic discipline, whether scholarly or scientific, requires reflection before it can be comprehended or elaborated. That observation does not deny the existence or the value of sudden flashes of insight enabling a theory to be formulated or improved, yet the gifted innovator undoubtedly possesses a wealth of relevant knowledge from which the insight has been derived and into which it is then embedded (Route 3b). For the moment consider philosophy which perhaps more than most scholarly disciplines stresses hesitation with almost maximum reflection. The values philosophers cultivate and ascribe to human beings require profound cogitation and cultivation. Examples abound, consider Unamuno as a typical illustration—or an atypical one, it matters not. Faith, he thinks, is "believing what we have not seen, no! but creating what we do not see. . . . And we create God—that is to say, God creates Himself in us—by compassion, by love." Then, too, "in order to love everything, in order to pity everything, human and extra-human, living and non-living, you must feel everything within yourself, you must personalize everything."[34] Principals with such faith, creativity, feelings, and empathy cannot be forever or frequently impulsive, they must continually hesitate and reflect as they construct their own existence rather than allowing themselves to be puppets succumbing to environmental opportunities. According to a philosophizing physician, "One cannot affirm that a given object is light in color without tacitly assuming that it might have been dark . . . one cannot say 'I perceive' without tacitly assuming a self-conscious, self-consistent, relatively continuous 'I.' "[35] Surely such thoughts are not likely either to occur or to be comprehended spontaneously and impulsively. Do you think that he who wishes to cultivate hesitancy should read philosophy? If so, will the reflection required by that evasive discipline generalize to other behavior? Implicitly some psychologists also similarly extol hesitation when they speak of "unfettered and open intercourse with the world" resulting in the individual's growth, insight, "a new vision," and inspiration.[36] Or could they be referring to poetry?

Perhaps the greatest advantage of hesitation with reflection rather than impulsivity is the increased probability of avoiding errors—not always, but often. Two psychologists have devised ingenious situations in which subjects, usually

American college students, but sometimes also Israeli children and students, have been asked challenging questions, the correct answers to which are not obvious. Here are three of their examples expressed in my words:

1. Usually the percentage of boys born in a hospital over time is around 50 percent; in which of two hospitals, one large and the other small, can it be anticipated that the percentage of boys in a period of days will be over 60 percent?

2. Does the letter "r" in English words occur more frequently as a first than as a third letter?

3. Is a robin a more typical bird than a chicken?[37]

(If you must hesitate concerning the correct answers, it can be revealed that the atypical 60 percent of boys is to be anticipated in the smaller hospital because the larger sample is less likely to stray from the expected value of 50 percent; the letter "r" occurs more frequently in third than in first place in spite of your ability to list the former more easily or readily than the latter; chickens may be more numerous than robins but their frequency is not necessarily related to their representativeness.) Yes, these are somewhat tricky intellectual exercises; yet they do more than tickle one's fancy as do some of the illustrations in the previous section of this chapter. Serious reflection is thus needed in order to avoid commonsense errors.

Some convincing evidence, though largely conventional, suggests that an increment of motivation is added as a result of "self-evaluation and self-efficacy mechanisms activated by cognitive comparison."[38] Self-evaluation and self-efficacy mean that the principal is preoccupied with his past, present, and future actions and is sensitive to his own "inner feelings."[39] Reflection of this sort, however, can make the principal less inclined to act, as illustrated by two items from a conventional attitude schedule: "I feel that I have very little to contribute to the welfare of others," "One soon learns to expect very little of other people."[40]

Any principle remains an abstraction until, after reflection, it is applied to a specific event and thus affects judgment and possibly behavior. Many persons in Western society believe or do not believe that they live in a just world.

Among the twenty items on a scale devised to assess that belief were such statements as "I've found that a person rarely deserves the reputation he has," "It is often impossible for a person to receive a fair trial in the U.S.A.," and "Crime doesn't pay." Perhaps those subscribing to the just world are therefore willing "to undertake socially beneficial activities, whether these be spending long years in school or obeying traffic laws."[41] The immediate judgments stemming from the just-world principle may be relatively quick, but the link between the event being judged and the judgment itself has required reflection in the past (Route 3a). May I ask, do you think that particular person deserves the reputation he has?

On the positive side, it is being argued, various virtues can be cultivated only by deliberately curbing impulsiveness and then by reflecting. A mere reference to "responsibility" immediately suggests that, although a principal may be able to appreciate without hesitation the decisions he must make or the actions he must pursue, often, maybe too often he must reflect before deciding or acting. Do you have any responsibility for the starving children in an African country? Hope and faith also epitomize virtues when they are not substitutes for procrastination. Instead of simply praising these human proclivities in general terms or hollow phrases, substitute the concept of planning. Hope is considered "the most general name we can give to the way we have access to the reality of a world of what ought to be." That definition comes from a Jesuit who therefore indicates that hope is "the power that worship has to form and to focus the public context of Christian understanding and practice." The expression of human values stems from the belief that human beings can cooperate and thereby shape their "moral future" and from the hope that we can make that future different from the past.[42] To reject the present or parts of it in favor of the future or parts of it demands courage, much hesitation, and reflection. Sometimes, however, in international affairs hesitation and procrastination achieve a political objective even when hesitation is not deliberate or not based upon reflection or leads to no action. Before the construction of the Berlin Wall, American officials took no action concerning devel-

opments in East Germany, and there was no war. After the
Wall was built, again the officials did nothing, on the basis
of which Soviet authorities may have inferred that the
American government was prepared to tolerate the existence
of East Germany, and there was no war. Eventually the Wall
was destroyed by the East Germans, and there was no war.

After any plan has been formulated, the planner must have
faith that it can be executed and that the conditions he has
postulated for its execution will be those he has anticipated.
Faith? Yes, a theological term again is needed. In fact, a theologian has collected empirical data concerning faith by interviewing a large number of informants, presumably Americans, and from sources depicting the lives of saints and saint-
like persons. When these individuals felt lost and especially
when they faced the certainty of death, they sought "a coat
against this nakedness," which was faith. For faith enabled
them not to succumb impulsively to despair; instead they
hesitated and somehow carried on. The same writer postu-
lates six stages in "faith development" that range from that
of infancy when the child is "influenced by example, words,
actions, and stories of the visible faith of primarily related
adults" to the "exceedingly rare" sixth stage of adulthood in
which there is "a disciplined, activist *incarnation*—a making
real and tangible—of the imperatives of absolute love and
justice."[43]

Faith may also be based upon the principal's own ability
and self-confidence. In a program designed to help adult
Americans abandon smoking, it was once found that a general belief ("When I have a strong urge for something such
as a cigarette or something sweet, I can resist the temptation") was more closely related to actually abstaining than
a specific belief ("Although it might be difficult, I am confident that I could quit smoking if I really put my mind to
it"). The general belief seems to refer to faith in the principal's ability "to cope," the more specific belief to faith in his
"will power,"[44] that is, to reflect rather than to be impulsive. To abandon smoking it seems that the general belief in
this instance was more action-determining than the specific
one.

Another attribute, also designated as faith, according to

one perspicacious author, "is the psychological process through which we suspend, or override, our rational ability and accept nonrational answers to our questions concerning life." Faith-destiny rather than determinism? The thesis is developed by reminding us that the motivating power behind faith, especially religious faith, is the fear that results from raising the questions that we ourselves have raised and for which we have found no answers; thus as victims of our own ability to reason we reduce the fear by means of faith. We do not immediately copulate, this writer also reminds us as if reminding were needed, in the manner of animals when the urge is upon us: "Most of the energy we spend on sex is not spent in actual coitus but in thinking, planning, and getting ready for it."[45] Faith, in brief, requires hesitation with reflection; the fear may be brushed aside, the impulse may be squelched, but eventually some solution is found. Really?

A negative, skeptical point—which by now is to be anticipated—is essential as the praise of considerable hesitation ends: such hesitation may result only from the principal's personal concerns and anxieties that cause him to avoid making decisions and to engage in appropriate action. Simple or complex worries about personal matters particularly with reference to the family, about successes and failures generally, or even about problems beyond one's control, such as environmental pollution, may be related to the principal's background factors that induce too much hesitation in the present (Route 3b).[46] Perhaps less reflection and more impulsivity with action is desirable. Such a proclivity to hesitate is difficult to overcome and may demand basic changes within the principal including even those resulting from psychotherapy. Changing degrees of hesitation involves basic tendencies relating to self-esteem, self-control, and other general or specific skills.[47] And so, gracefully, the next chapter is introduced.

IN SHORT: definitely, quite definitely, impulsivity is usually branded as undesirable and reflection is deluged with praise; relatively rarely, moreover, do the two extreme degrees of hesitation receive and merit the reverse evaluation.

8

Training

We ever strive to live better lives by improving our environments, our society, and ourselves. Sometimes we are helpless: the earthquake erupts or the drought persists, and there is little we can do except to hope, pray, or invoke a relevant fate-destiny doctrine. An inflation or a war breaks out and we adjust as best we can, but rarely to our complete satisfaction. A similarly dismal situation may exist with reference to ourselves: the traumas we have endured in the past continue to haunt us; like guilt, we cannot shake them away from our everyday life or from our dreams. But we do think we know that we can at least attempt to improve ourselves either by altering the forces that affect us or those over which we believe we have direct control. The invocation endeth; we now have the courage to try to curb impulsivity most of the time and to cultivate reflection part of the time.

A moment's reflection indicates the need to reflect in order to examine the basis for many judgments that are accepted uncritically. In recalling the past history of an individual or in reading the history of a group or society, the principal is confronted with a number of alternatives. Which have been the significant events being recalled or recounted and for what reasons should they be considered significant? What are the labels attached to those events or in what kind of language, laudatory or not, are they expressed? How are the events grouped together? For the individual, at what point does he make a distinction between adolescence and adulthood? For the historian, what justification does he provide for dividing his account into eras? The observer, unless he is generally skeptical or unless he is a trained therapist or historian, may accept an account without reflecting, without challenging the selection of events and the labels; it is not easy to hesitate concerning a given account or any account and then reflect critically.

Will, can, may, must, or should we train ourselves or be trained to decrease impulsivity and to increase reflection? That omnibus question has already been considered in part. We may not hesitate to pay taxes, and the penalties imposed by government compel us not to hesitate too long or to procrastinate—well, we do hesitate and reflect as we fill out the tax forms or select the items to be taxed. Or my well worn illustrations: we cannot hesitate to blink or cringe when the appropriate stimulus reaches our sense organs. "Involuntary" hesitation also occurs when visual or auditory stimulation outlasts the actual stimulation from the external source.[1] Otherwise, except when decisions and reactions stem from completely external situations or constraints, we must assume that the values inherent in all the Critical Questions are more likely to be salient during reflection than during relatively rapid impulsiveness. How can reflective judgments and actions be cultivated, what modes of training can be recommended? Here is one person's opinion, mine, grounded whenever possible in the experience of which you and I are aware when we contemplate those experiences. And yet I hesitate for more than a moment to recommend more hesitation or reflection. I cannot forget, as I have already said, the joy of spontaneity which, though impulsive, can occur without troubling to consider all the questions and without committing a moral blunder. "Almost no one, including physicists, engineers, bicycle manufacturers," according to a trio of psychologists, "can communicate the strategy whereby a cyclist keeps his balance. The underlying principle would not really be of much help even if they did know how to express it."[2] But we do learn to cycle, and off we go with little hesitation. We may even take courage from the most varied relations, from robust to "trivial", between the ability of some American subjects to delay gratification in experimentally manipulated conditions;[3] training of that sort at the very least may be considered feasible.

Before offering prescriptions to improve reflection, however, a skeptical note must be struck twice. First, we know that curbing impulsivity sometimes may be difficult or impossible. Talkative persons believe that they always have something significant to say, and therefore they cannot or will not curb themselves from initiating or interrupting conversations. When a group of "normal" and "emotionally disturbed" boys undergoing psychiatric treatment once performed a series of exercises involving motor inhibitions, estimating when thirty seconds had elapsed, and also answering questions concerning delayed gratification, the disturbed children could work rapidly and with abandon "but when they were asked to restrain their energies and to inhibit their motor responses they [fared] less well than the normal children."[4] The so-called psychotic individual epitomizes the tragic consequences that can be associated with impulsivity: he may require careful and prolonged psychiatric treatment before he improves, but the improvement may be incomplete or temporary.

Then, secondly, there is no sure-fire way to achieve more or less reflection, more or less impulsivity. The technique must be adapted to the principals at hand, including their previous tendencies to hesitate. In addition, we have no one completely reliable guide book to consult. We have at our disposal literally thousands of psychiatric and psychological studies as well as the experiences of countless psychiatrists and clinical psychologists and therapists; at the same time, at least in the United States, men and women in the press, over the radio, and on television spontaneously advise those troubled by personal problems. Are such sages fakes; are they to be condemned as glib quacks? Perhaps not: in giving spontaneous advice to the lovelorn, the obese, the drug addicted, and others in difficulties they are using their common sense buttressed or not in systematic studies or disciplines and based, as is often the case, on their own intuitive experiences. Neither they nor we can consult computer printouts revealing the "best" or most desirable advice to offer those in distress; all of us would remain silent and useless if compelled to search and search before offering counsel. Perhaps we come closer to "better" advice when our suggestions stem from acceptable research and "experts"— perhaps. I have thus explained and offer an excuse for the remainder of this chapter.

External Guides

An external device that calls attention to the rules or values governing a situation can facilitate reflection. Posting the legal speed limit on a road sign is a crude but usually effective warning to motorists who thus are reminded of a regulation requiring obedience or, if ignored, leading to possible punishment. Years ago a sign on a busy highway between Lagos and Ibadan in Nigeria, if I remember it correctly, stimulated additional and perhaps more enduring reflection among English-speakers when it proclaimed, "Better be Late, Mister, than the Late Mister." External guides of this sort, however, can become part of the landscape and then no longer provoke additional reflection. Does the sight of a cross on a church do more than remind the passerby of the religious denomination or the building's function? Does it induce him to reflect upon the values of Christianity?

The absence of external stimulation that facilitates impulsivity may be useful. If you wish to give up smoking, you do not carry a package of cigarettes in your pocket or purse— unless you wish to demonstrate the strength of your resolution or character to other persons and yourself. You make the cigarettes less easily available so that you do not impulsively reach for one and so that you must at least hesitate a bit to go to the trouble to fetch one. But, alas, the desire to smoke, being repressed, may eventually burst forth; abandoning an old habit is not easy.

Models are or can be important as external guides because, some evidence suggests,[5] curbing impulsivity may occur when principals are taught consciously to adopt a stance adapted to the situation at hand. The guide may be another person who seeks to affect the principal for his own good or who functions as a model for that principal to follow. Wittingly or unwittingly David prevented the heavily armed and superior Philistine Goliath from impulsively slaying him by pitching the encounter on a verbal level. First Goliath, noting that David was *"but* a youth,"* immediately not only "disdained him" but also abused him, "Am I a dog, that thou comest to me with staves?" Then David hurled a much longer barrage of words at his opponent ("I come to thee in the name of the Lord of hosts"), immediately after which the unarmed David was able to slay the presumably distracted Goliath with a "stone that sunk into his forehead."[6]

The model promoting reflection must have either authority or prestige. Up to a point parents influence their children by their own behavior as well as by the values they transmit, deliberately or not, in words. The patient who voluntarily consults a psychiatrist in order to understand and then learn to control unsatisfactory impulsive behavior has selected a figure whose advice he supposedly is willing to follow. "Strong" evidence once possibly indicated conventionally that subjects could be "persuaded and influenced" and convinced to perform feared acts, such as touching a snake, after "therapeutic instructions" concerning fear or "pseudotherapies" concerning physiological processes.[7] Presumably such desensitizing training altered anticipations of what would occur in the anxiety-producing situation and hence diminished hesitation. Psychoanalysts and other psychiatrists, however, agree with these findings that there is no rapid, infallible technique to desensitize the fears of many patients who therefore continue to hesitate to plunge into situations that unrealistically appear dangerous to them.

Teachers in school necessarily enforce some kind of discipline in order to be able to teach; thus their charges learn, more or less, to inhibit or delay some of their impulses. Various techniques have been employed with moderate and fluctuating success. One review of the experimental studies points to four different pedagogical methods. Children have been forced to delay their response when confronted with alternatives. They have been reinforced with praise when they responded correctly. They have listened to adults or peers who indicated the desirability or greater efficiency of delay. Or they have been impressed with the desirability of scanning and been taught how to scan alternatives before arriving at a judgment.[8] Among these American children it appears as if forced delay was the least effective method and that modelling and scanning were more effective.

The details of each impulsivity-reducing technique require special attention. In one experiment it was direct training pertaining to delay that decreased impulsivity, yet gaining rapport with the child by saying that the adult and he or she shared common interests and characteristics made no significant difference.[9] Kindergarten and second-grade children were once first given the Matching Test; then ten days later the test was repeated after they had received one of three different instructions which in effect asked them to be as accurate as possible, to find the correct drawing as quickly as possible, or simply to do the best they could. Here changes in impulsivity were related not only to the method of instruction (those receiving the accuracy instruction, for example, tended to make fewer errors the second time than those receiving the best-you-can exhortation), but also both to their initial scores on the test and their ages.[10] In these studies, we need to be reminded that the improvement or changes have depended on the method of measuring hesitation. The Matching Test was once employed as the measure when a sample of disabled children learned to follow the example of a model who employed silent or inner speech as a guide to solving a visual problem; their performance on that particular test improved but not their own self-esteem or the impulsivity ratings given them by their classroom teachers.[11] In another study the same test was given to both the teachers and their first-grade pupils: between the autumn and the spring the children with reflective teachers as their model, especially the boys, became more reflective, as indicated by an increase in their response time to that test, but not their accuracy.[12]

Often adequate reflection depends upon both external guides and internal beliefs or attitudes.[13] Originally the child is restrained by a parent from darting across a busy street to see a friend; it is hoped that he never again will have an inclination to succumb to such an impulse, and that he will appreciate the danger and recall the parental warning. But later will he actually come to appreciate the connection between the impulse and its consequence? Or an adult decides not to buy certain luxury items because they are too expensive at a time of high taxation; subsequently he avoids external temptation by not reading certain advertisements or by not window-shopping at certain stores.

Anticipations

In Western society, and possibly all societies, parents know they must love their children and protect them; and ordinarily they unhesitatingly do just that. Eventually in varying degrees these children would and actually do become independent; they follow their own wishes by and large and do not expect to seek approval for all their formal actions from their parents or to be obedient to them. At this point in the lives of parents, according to one psychiatrist, "patience and fortitude now become the watchwords replacing demonstrative love, support, and discipline as symbols of helpful parenthood."[14] Parental impulse gives rise to hesitation accompanied by reflection as rules change. Perhaps— yes, the word *perhaps* must be added—the adjustment is less painful or even satisfying if the details can be anticipated.

Every event and hence every situation has a temporal dimension that may be brief or extended. Even when the principal is totally relaxed—he is listening to music or only half awake—he knows that the interval will end; if questioned, he may hesitate to designate the exact moment when it will end, yet he will try to anticipate what will come next. Ordi-

narily the role of anticipation immediately before impulsive
actions may be fleeting or unconscious: if I don't do this right
now, all hell will break loose. The anticipation of the consequences, as one of the Critical Questions suggests, can evoke
incentives to attain or avoid them; more generally, "The evidence that expectancies influence attention is comparatively
strong,"[15] and attention means salience, hesitation, and perhaps reflection.[16]

Often, however, all or most of the details cannot be anticipated. What does a boxer do concerning the strategy he will
use against an opponent he has never met?[17] He learns what
he can from reports concerning the man and, when available, photographs or films. Before the bout he may reflect
concerning the best strategy or even the tactics to employ,
but he must wait until the match begins when he then seeks
to implement his plans either impulsively or, depending on
what his opponent does, somewhat impulsively with little
hesitation (Route 3a).

More socially significant planning resembles boxing, any
other sport entailing face-to-face competition, and especially
chess. The principal anticipates as much as he can but must
be ever prepared to change as situations develop. Can the
principal anticipate what his role in a crisis will be? There
may be a tendency to believe that unpleasant events, such
as being robbed, suffering an accident, or developing cancer
are less likely to occur to oneself than to others; yet some
preparation is essential. Flight attendants routinely instruct
their passengers concerning what they can or must do in case
of an emergency, but their audience probably is inattentive
by and large because they wish to consider their plane safe
and because they prefer not to dwell on morbid matters. Fire
drills in schools and other public buildings simulate the actions to be taken when-and-if and hence then to avoid impulsive panic. Morbidity rather than steady foresight, however, may accompany anticipation. A sample of Polish female
students living within the range of the increased radiation
resulting from the explosion of the atomic power plant at
Chernobyl, for example, anticipated that their own chances
of becoming victims of similar accidents were less than for

other persons; they anticipated that the possibility of suffering health problems from the radiation were greater; thus in
a realistic setting they were "unrealistically pessimistic" about
themselves.[18]

Utilization of Past Experience

If the Critical Questions are to receive valid and morally
desirable replies, past experience as a guide for present and
future impulsivity and reflection must be utilized with extreme caution. On the one hand, human beings should profit
from the hesitancies of the past so that they can select the
best route for present purposes. On the other hand, the future is never quite like the past so that innovative judgments
or actions are essential. This axiomatic truism may provoke
a polite rebuff or a sneer, yet it merits the most serious concern if the degree of hesitation at the moment is to be fruitful.

Historians, the professional ones, must deliberate before
they deliver their version of past events. One of them indicates the somewhat self-evident perils they must and do not
necessarily overcome: the very question they pose to investigate, the ways in which they claim to verify their interpretations, and the "facts" or events they must select to report
must inevitably bias the account they present.[19] And so, according to another member of the craft, "no historian should
ever pretend that he has achieved a 'definitive interpretation' of that great mystery which is human life, in all its
variety and diversity, in all its misery and grandeur, in its
ambiguity and contradictions, in its basic 'freedom.' "[20] If
professionals so frankly admit their troubles with interpreting the past, then the rest of us must modestly wonder which
of their versions to accept as we ponder the future. Or do we
actually trouble ourselves to cope more or less successfully
with the identical problem?

Non-historians may subscribe to views of the past which,
when tested, are not necessarily valid. One of the "longest-
held beliefs" of persons settling the American West during
the nineteenth century was that the glorious opportunities

they sought there had disappeared shortly before their arrival and hence they were a "few moments late for the party."[21] In order to feel less frustrated by this gloomy perception of reality, these pioneers had to ignore their misconception and reap what benefits they could from the present.

Even though diverse situations in the future will not exactly duplicate ones in the past, it would be foolish not to invoke the past as at least a tentative guide to the future. Principals sensibly make such an assumption without or with some risk, so that later they can react desirably with little hesitation (Routes 2a or 3a). They set an alarm clock to be awakened at an hour of their selection; they avoid a street that has acquired a dubious reputation, animals that might attack them, persons who are likely to humiliate them;[22] they know when to use a mathematical or a moral principle in order to resolve a "new" problem. An individual does not hesitate whether to swim across a swiftly moving river even when he wishes to reach the other side because he knows that he will be unable to cope with the current: he once tried to swim against a less violent stream without success, or he has been told that this particular stream is dangerous. She has rules of her own to which she adheres; she hesitates to make crucial decisions when she is fatigued or in a depressed mood, for she has taught herself that decisions under those conditions have seldom been propitious. Procrastination can thus be productive. Similarly, patience may be cultivated when the individual realizes that impulsive decisions in the past have been unwise. Past experience may thus be at the basis of actions that appear to observers to be impulsive but are really the fruition of what has been previously judged or done (variable linkage). A venerable physiologist suggests that inspiration has its origin in "a wide knowledge of the facts." "In typical cases," he adds, "a hunch appears after a long study and springs into consciousness at a time when the investigator is not working on his problem."[23]

Experience, however, also requires that the praise of experience be restrained, inasmuch as the past can be a misleading or disabling manual for the future. That future, I repeat, is more often than not somewhat different from the past and hence the differences must be noted: the alarm clock may have to be reset, the dangerous street may now be well guarded by the police, and the scientific principle does not seem relevant to some new, puzzling situation. Young children may find it difficult or impossible to hesitate in situations for which they have once or frequently found solutions in the past; possibly they may "rarely" be able before the age of eight to judge phrases or sentences describing events they have not experienced.[24] Instead of being impulsive, therefore, principals who receive adequate so-called feedback should hesitate and pause to determine precisely how they can profit from the information. Reflection may enable them to puncture their inevitable stereotypes concerning other persons and situations and then reject the past experience with the result that they may be able to avoid overgeneralization and appreciate and assess the uniqueness of each person and situation. Even the "well-educated" may believe they can attribute various characteristics to other healthy males and females when they know only that such persons are "traditional" or "liberated";[25] were they to pause a bit more than a moment or two, they might be in a position to recognize the individuality of the individuals upon whom the glib labels are glibly plastered. In truly a basic sense, therefore, past experiences must be utilized creatively by both principals and observers, especially since frequently new information is required before judgments at the moment are passed (Route 3b).[26]

In at least one sense principals use past experience to create their own futures not only by deciding to reach goals that have previously eluded them but also by then conforming to their own predictions. The latter, nowadays called a "self-fulfilling prophecy," is illustrated by depositors in a bank who believe the bank is going to fail and hence help cause it to fail by withdrawing or trying to withdraw their deposits. In contrast is the "self-destroying belief": the belief that the bank will fail is proven to be false because its directors then receive financial assistance from a government agency or because some potent depositors do not withdraw funds but increase their deposits to prevent its failure.[27] In both instances a belief leads to intervention by producing or preventing the predicted consequence. On the basis of what you have read in the past, do you agree that it is difficult—impossible?—for the psychological and social sciences to be scientific since their subject matter, human beings, can affect the very predictions those disciplines evolve? Similarly school teachers who believe that some pupils are bright and others dull either may vindicate their beliefs by grading them accordingly or they will pay more attention to the bright than to the dull children. They may also make extra efforts to help those they believe to be dull, and then the students in turn will come to react accordingly, so that those considered bright will have more self-confidence and those hypothesized as dull will become less self-confident.[28]

Awareness of Mistakes

The members of every society, now or in the past, are deluged with maxims, proverbs, commandments, aphorisms, epigrams and other bits of wisdom that usually appear banal but that seek to serve as guides to achieve the moral and avoid the immoral: haste makes waste, don't put off till tomorrow what you can do today, a stitch in time saves nine, and so on. Some of this wisdom can function as an internal rather than an external guide in the cultivation of hesitation accompanying reflection. Throughout the ages both sages and quacks have offered suggestions concerning ways to avoid the fallacies associated with impulsivity. A skeptical devil's advocate, nevertheless, doth quickly find in Bartlett "Live while ye may" (Milton), "When pleasure can be had, it is fit to catch it" (Samuel Johnson), "He who can does; he who cannot teaches" (G. B. Shaw), and perhaps another long string.[29]

But, back on the main track, fleeing from impulsivity, one might begin with Aristotle whose guides to correct syllogistic reasoning can be learned, perhaps even by college sophomores, and thereafter utilized to challenge both the premises from which deductions are made and then the deductions themselves. The roster of advisers who advocate ways to avoid impulsivity and to reflect more frequently would include most philosophers, many psychiatrists and psychologists, and—at least by implication—the more skillful dramatists and novelists. The majority of Christians in the West who attend church next Sunday will also be offered hints by their ministers who call attention to incorrect interpretations of scripture and the failure of some members of the congregation to follow the principles of the religion to which they ostensibly adhere. A series of fat volumes would be required to list and evaluate the suggestions advocated by leaders of most religions and sects everywhere to interested and disinterested audiences who, they assert or imply, have succumbed to the impulsive temptations offered by the evil one and who are then urged to tread the indicated paths to righteousness. One quick way to sample this vast and often contradictory literature is to consider, first, a set of "fallacies" people allegedly are prone to commit and propaganda "devices" allegedly leading them astray and then, second, to glance at experimental studies.

The political philosopher Jeremy Bentham groups human fallacies under four headings, defined and illustrated as follows:

1. *Fallacies of Authority*: "to repress all exercise of the reasoning faculty" and specifically to adduce "authority in various shapes as conclusive upon the subject of the measure proposed." For example: references to "our wise ancestors—the wisdom of our ancestors—the wisdom of ages—venerable antiquity—wisdom of old times."

2. *Fallacies of Danger*: "to repress discussions altogether by exciting alarm" and hence "to draw aside attention from the *measure* to the *man*." For example: "Of no measure can anybody be sure, but that it may be followed by some other measure or measures, of which, when they make their appearance, it may be said that they are bad."

3. *Fallacies of Delay*: "to postpone discussion, with a view to eluding it." For example: "Wait a little, this is not the time."

4. *Fallacies of Confusion*: "to perplex, when Discussion can no longer be avoided." For example: "Substituting for men's proper offi-

cial denomination the names of some fictitious entity, to whom, by customary language, and thence opinion, the attribute of excellence has been attached."

Indeed, Bentham's classificatory system is most impressively packaged with illustrations of the fallacies that he detected during his lifetime and that can be too easily illustrated a century and a half later. His "practical conclusion" concerning those fallacies is that "in proportion as the acceptance and thence the utterance of them can be prevented, the understanding of the public will be strengthened, the morals of the public will be purified, and the practice of government improved."[30] It should be evident, I add, that to recognize and not be misled by a fallacy, even the third one that inveighs against unnecessary delay or procrastination, requires the principal to pause, to hesitate, to reflect, and thus to evaluate the misleading argument confronting him.

A more modern labelling device was employed by the Institute for Propaganda Analysis during the half decade right before the United States entered World War II. The general purpose was to make students in secondary schools and the general public aware of the propaganda devices being employed to influence them; the much less explicit objective was to prevent principals from succumbing to the kind of propaganda which, in the opinion of many of us organizers, had misled Americans to enter World War I—were we wrong both times? A manual defined and illustrated the snappy, easily memorizable, more or less self-explanatory titles of the devices: name calling, glittering generality, testimonial, plain folks, card stacking, band wagon, and transfer (of authority or prestige from the respectable or revered to render another referent respectable).[31] After adding the terms to their vocabulary and after practicing them, it was assumed that principals would recognize their presence in the communications of the day, would then stop and reflect, and not be seduced. Somewhat similarly, it has been proposed that recalling slogans derived from findings in social science may induce principals to reflect: "It's an empirical question";

"Which hat did you draw that sample out of?"; "Okay, what do the other three" possibilities suggest?; Have you considered the principal's "situation before jumping to conclusions about his dispositions?"[32]

In recent times a catchy, semi-neologism "groupthink" has been employed to designate the faulty decisions that may result when a small, "cohesive" group, especially of congenial persons, strives to achieve unanimity or does so by downplaying or ignoring realistic alternatives and hence spends inadequate time weighing those alternatives. One incident now called "classic" was the American decision to invade Cuba in 1961—the Bay of Pigs fiasco—in which the advisers were swayed by their devotion to President Kennedy and hence did not consider adequately the possibility of disaster or other ways besides force to affect the Cuban government. Victims of groupthink impulsively give a higher priority to personal loyalties and rapport within their small group than they do to the realities confronting them. According to the originator of the conception, the penalties of groupthink can be avoided by facilitating additional hesitation: have more than one group work on the problem, spend ample time surveying alternatives, and schedule at least a second meeting to reconsider the decision at which "residual doubts" are deliberately raised and the issue is rethought.[33]

Now to the experimenting psychologists. The investigators mentioned in the previous chapter who in effect have implied that reflection is required if one is to decide in which hospital more boys than girls were born, the frequency of the letter "r" as the first or third letter in English words, and the typicality of robins and chickens have conducted and inspired experiments in which numerous errors are convincingly portrayed. In this tradition, three investigators indicate the errors people may commit when they reply to the question, "Does God answer prayers?" If they say "Yes" and offer confirmatory evidence, they may be neglecting three other empirical possibilities: they prayed and their prayers were not answered; they did not pray and obtained what they sought; and they did not pray and did not obtain what they sought.[34] Before replying to questions less lofty such as those involving cause and effect, the principal would do well to consider all four possibilities.

In the same tradition other American psychologists have uncovered the kinds of errors committed, usually impulsively, by their subjects. Principals, they note, have a tendency to draw an inference from a single instance; he must be bright, he answered my questions quickly. Their judgment may result from what they themselves have done; after being rude to him, they think his subsequent rudeness indicates that he is a rude person. They are convinced that their personal impressions are more valid than records or factual information; he made a very favorable impression on me when I met him, which was quite contrary to what his friends and acquaintances have reported.[35] They overpraise hindsight; she should have been able to anticipate what happened.[36] They fail to utilize or ignore relevant information; that will not happen because the situation now is quite different. They have confidence in haphazard or illustrative samples; this has never happened to people I know.[37] In effect we have here rules to be obeyed if impulsive errors are to be eschewed. But at the spur of the moment will or can principals remember the rules?

Other experiments are concerned with modes of communication. It has been demonstrated that two devices are likely to facilitate cooperation from unsuspecting principals who may be called victims in this context. One is the foot-in-the-door technique: a trivial request most likely to produce compliance is followed by a lesser request actually desired by the dominating observer; for example, have the principal answer a few innocent questions, which he does willingly, before asking him to do you a favor or buy the product you are selling. The other is the door-in-the-face approach: after, as expected, an outrageous request has been rejected, then make the more reasonable request, the one the observer really seeks to have granted; for example, urge the principal to join and actively participate in a charitable organization before asking him to contribute a small sum of money to that organization. Either technique, it has once been demonstrated conventionally, when the objective was to obtain assistance, has

produced less hesitation when it was accompanied by a specific request than when such a request had not been made;
without the request, the door-in-the-face approach may possibly produce slightly faster cooperation than the foot-in-the-
door approach.[38] Investigators may be pursuing a will-o'-the-
wisp as they compare the two approaches, however, because
too much depends on the nature of the request and the mode
of communication (whether face-to-face or by telephone). Thus
the foot-in-the-door technique was once found to be ineffec-
tive when a sample of adult Americans, having answered
questions pertaining to health practices, was asked later to
answer a longer list concerning common household products, regardless of whether they were reminded of the first
or smaller request, whether the second request was relatively small or large, or whether that second request was
made after an elapsed time ranging from one day to three
weeks.[39]

Inhabitants of modern societies are swamped with advertisements proclaiming the virtues of almost every imagin-
able product. Accompanying this flood have been experimental investigations seeking to demonstrate some of the
devices likely to be effective. A knowledge of these devices
could be a form of inoculation that might prevent consumers
from being influenced and hence deceived or swindled. Consider whether a communication should be one-sided or offer
negative or doubtful arguments as well as positive ones. Fairly
copious evidence among North Americans indicates that two-
sided messages enhance credibility but not necessarily the
affective response.[40] Perhaps principals can thus be warned
concerning the hazards of impulsive gullibility.

And now the usual warning and pinch of skepticism:
awareness of fallacies, propaganda devices, the traps set by
do-gooders or evil-doers, and the logical errors of undergraduates may stimulate hesitation and reflection but dare not
be considered a panacea. For the principal who has been told
or knows that what he feels or judges is fallacious or neurotic may be unable to curb his impulse to commit the error.
Knowing that hypochondriacal individuals employ their alleged illnesses or symptoms to account for their poorer

performances[41] does not automatically prevent you or me
from conveniently employing the device: I really feel sick,
you must excuse me, I'm just not up to it. For the same reason psychiatric assistance requires more than the communication of a diagnosis and suggested therapy: the patient
must interiorize the information, reflect in order to gain insight into himself and his difficulty, and then perhaps be able
to change. Sometimes training must be specific: the evidence possibly indicates that in situations like the Matching
Test principals can be taught to react more slowly but that
the accuracy of their responses may not be affected unless
they are also given instruction on how to be more accurate.[42]
Also it has been shown, conventionally and over short periods of time, that principals who are provided with information about the ways in which they can be manipulated
may or may not acquire immunity; the effect of prior tutor-
ing turns out to be "highly variable."[43] Somehow, therefore,
principals must be convinced or convince themselves that
they control events or at least some of what happens to them,
for without that conviction they become anxious and assume
they cannot avoid frustration or disaster.[44]

Self-Control

Nobody, except the adherents of a faith who postulate and
worship a divine being that once appeared or will appear
again in human form, is able and willing to designate the
perfect attributes of the perfect person. All that humble mortals can do is to point diffidently to traits that appear related
to an ability to raise and respond adequately to the Critical
Questions. Here the task is even humbler: to designate self-
control quite arbitrarily as a disposition that can be cultivated, perhaps, perhaps, and that is capable of promoting
greater hesitation and reflection as well as the ability to distinguish between destructive and fruitful impulsiveness.

First, however, it must be noted that hesitation with reflection occurs only when the principal is active, when he
consciously is seeking some goal; it is much less likely when
he feels "bored." Boredom means that either adequate stim-

ulation may be lacking or else similar stimulation is repeated again and again.[45] Are you bored when you are alone or when your good friend keeps telling you the same story over and over? One of the accompaniments of loneliness, the cause-or-effect sequences of which have been previously mentioned, may be boredom; in contrast solitude can provide the opportunity for reflection when the principal has hesitated to reach a decision or when he seeks to be creative. Falling asleep or wishing to do so is often one of the consequences of boredom. The bored person has ceased to control the relation between his self and either his external or internal environment.

"Obviously" a psychologist declaims, "self-control is a good thing to have"[46]—and he is probably correct when one contemplates the frequent postponements required in any society. Any parent must renounce some immediate joy for himself in favor of the child whose welfare and growth he would protect. You must plant potatoes, you must study, you must put aside capital now if you are to prosper in the future. The same writer reminds us, as if that were necessary, that we endure momentary agony in a dentist's chair in order to avoid more lasting pain in the future. But he also admits that we have "little to say" concerning how self-control in general can be acquired. He wonders, and so do we, whether giving up smoking is easier for a principal who has previously controlled his eating habits in order to reduce his weight or the amount of cholesterol in his blood stream than another person who has not learned how to abandon a well-established habit. Still we realize that all values, those involving the highest moral values as well as physical health, can seldom be achieved in a flash: Critical Questions must be asked and answered, hesitation with or without reflection is required.

Control is needed if past experience is not to be misapplied in the manner of egocentric or ethnocentric stereotypes. Is that view just a stereotype I have concerning people who live in some foreign country I have or have not visited, are they really so or have I acquired a biased view of them? Stereotypes can be so insidious that they cannot be easily cast aside. A significant relation was once found in Wales,

for example, between teachers' ratings of the physical attractiveness of their eleven- to twelve-year old pupils and
the following: their ratings of the children's leadership, confidence, popularity, academic brightness, and sociability.
These attractiveness ratings tended also to agree somewhat
(if not impressively) with the ratings by the investigators,
the ratings of photographs by five adults, and even the children's own ratings concerning themselves.[47] To be noted only
is the probability that the judgments of the behavioral attributes, valid or not, were made; the teachers may have failed
to reflect concerning the individuality of their charges.

The very notion of stereotype suggests that self-control is
not being exercised: a view, a belief, an attitude is applied
uncritically to selected segments of the referent; a "nothing-
but fallacy" is being committed. Is science—good, hard natural science—nothing but an attempt to predict the future
and retrodict the past? No, not unless crude actuarial reasoning is employed; otherwise, as philosophers of science are
keen to point out,[48] explanation and understanding are also
required. What is glibly called an open mind is necessary, if
nothing-buts are to be avoided. Always wide open? Even at
election time when we must vote, even though there is the
possibility that we do not know all that should or could be
known concerning the candidate or candidates who do not
meet our favor? Generalization and exceptions go hand in
hand; control must be exercised to determine in each instance which guide to employ.

President Calvin Coolidge allegedly once asserted that
"when people are out of work, unemployment results."[49] A
weary glance at that sentence might lead someone—not you,
not me—to believe that he was securing immediate insight
into one of the country's major problems, but then a moment of hesitation can produce the laughter or sneer the dec-
laration merits. Even laughter must be controlled until the
redundancy is grasped.

Efforts have been made to teach self-control in order to
curb impulsivity. One teacher sorted pictures in front of
American children, grades 2 to 4, who had been observed to
be hyperactive and underachieving. For the experimental

group she made statements that included, "find out what I am supposed to do," "consider all answers," "stop and think," "mark my answer," and "check my answer." After the pupils themselves had verbalized their own processes, they were told to convert them to covert or silent speech. Still later they were given a bonus if correct. Seven sessions were required. The scores on the Matching Test improved after this experience; and "many" showed improvement after ten months.[50] Do not for a moment, however, imagine that nirvana has been attained through the use of that method: earlier experiments with Canadian children in grades 1 and 2 which employed a similar approach and the same Matching Test reported a consequent decrease in latency but—as in another study mentioned in the section on External Guides—not in number of errors; also there was no difference in observed classroom behavior.[51] The accuracy of the responses of some but not all kindergarten and other young Israeli children to the Matching Test were improved after they had been deliberately trained on how to cope with such a test: they were taught to find figures similar to or different from the model, or to concentrate upon details or the entire configuration of that model.[52] In general terms, then, the impulsive principal must be made to recognize—presumably through deliberate probing and self-monitoring—that he himself can control his own impulsive *me*, which means that his "anticipations, expectations, and directedness" are revised instead of being subject to "undifferentiated" tension.[53]

Deliberately doing nothing or procrastinating requires self-control and may have significant moral consequences. In international negotiations, for example, delays may be productive: the protagonists can reconsider their positions, do little, or do nothing. Perhaps, for example, the most productive hesitation of our era since 1945 or so has been detente, particularly with reference to the use of nuclear weapons. On the other hand, it may be argued that some hesitation may produce undesirable results: the principal anticipates falsely short-term gains or long-term adverse effects.

Let us admit again our fallibility regarding ways to curb impulsivity. Plentiful are the instances in which well-controlled persons suddenly find themselves out of control or burst into action they themselves have previously scorned. Defective diagnoses of the popular lie detector have been previously mentioned. I was so annoyed I just had to tell him what I thought of him. Shame?

Many, perhaps most psychiatrists treat not symptoms but the personality as a whole, and of course not always successfully. Very arbitrarily let one report be examined. Borderline patients were hospitalized a minimum of six months, some for more than twelve months. During their sojourn there they were assigned to therapy groups; they attended meetings of the hospital community; they established friendly and informal relations with members of the staff; in short, they were treated humanely and given major assistance on a psychological level. Their symptoms were noted both upon admission and, when possible, one and two years after being discharged. "Impulsivity" was assessed by recording their suicidal or self-destructive feelings and their behavior in these respects as well as their tendency toward drug or alcohol abuse. Yes, there was a decrease in the percentage possessing these three symptoms; but for many the symptoms remained. For example: 82 percent revealed the indicated feelings upon admission, 60 percent a year and two years after discharge (corresponding figures for their behavior were a reduction from 65 to 30 and 25 percent, and for drug and alcohol abuses from 57 to 33 and 40 percent).[54] Admittedly there was no control group of patients or persons who did not receive the treatment and were not hospitalized; still there seems to have been a decrease in impulsivity as here defined for some but not for an appreciable number of the patients.

This therapeutic experience encountered a minor, practical difficulty: all the patients could not be located a year or two after being released from the hospital and hence the data are incomplete. The same problem also arises when principals voluntarily receiving therapeutic treatment simply drop out of the program and there is no way to compel them to continue to participate. A fifteen-week program combined "affective educational and social skills training" (via lectures, discussions, written exercises, games, role-playing, and other modes of interaction) in an effort to increase the self-esteem of outpatient American delinquents between the ages of 15 and 17. Over a three-year period, the course was repeated with different groups of adolescents. Only 6 out of 13 completed the course the first time; and the figures for the other three years were 9 out of 12, 7 out of 9, and 6 out of 7.[55] Was the venture worth the effort?

Psychologists conducting research on methods of curbing impulsivity, unless they are clinically oriented, tend to focus upon symptoms or specific actions rather than the total personality. A behavioristic and morally conscious psychologist once listed nine ways to achieve self-control: physical restraint (lock the door; increase taxation); change the stimulus (look away; sugar-coat the pill); deprive and satiate (drink water instead of whiskey; exercise instead of making love); manipulate emotional conditions (bite your tongue when laughter is inappropriate; rehearse privately what you are going to say); use aversive stimulation (set the alarm clock out of reach; add a bad taste to the cigarette); try drugs; resort to conditioning (promise yourself something attractive when the unattractive task is complete; do not repair the television set); punish yourself (tighten your belt so that you do not overeat; note your violations of a moral code); and do something else (change the topic of conversation; practice being decent). The author himself notes that these techniques may not work, the principal may backslide; and he finally places responsibility upon external rather than internal guides by arguing that "society is responsible for the larger part of the behavior of self-control."[56]

Another psychologist considers first how the legendary hero Odysseus prevented himself and his crew from succumbing impulsively to the alluring Sirens: he ordered them to tie him to the mast and not release him until they had sailed past; he then could only hear their alluring voices; the crews' ears he plugged with wax so that they could row and not be diverted by the inviting sounds. The same writer calls special attention to "private side bets" which a principal can also make with himself to control impulsivity: he can take a solemn oath not to be impulsive and perhaps invoke "the help of some sacred entity"; he can decide to act impulsively only when someone else does so; he can promise himself a larger reward in the future by abstaining from enjoying a smaller one in the present; or he can simply determine to exercise self-control through an act of will. The individual, however, may easily lose any of these bets; William James is cited in this context, "How many excuses does the drunkard find when each new temptation arises!"[57] The advocates of slogans as a way of curbing impulsivity gloomily and realistically likewise remind their readers that "knowledge of inferential principles and findings, and skill in applying that knowledge, does not guarantee correct inferences."[58]

Even though the principal may lose a private bet and forget a commanding slogan, some evidence suggests that changes engineered by himself may sometimes be more successful than those devised by outsiders.[59] It must be noted, too, that change of any sort almost always requires self-monitoring: the principal must reflect concerning the error of his ways in the past as well as the techniques enabling him perhaps to alter himself. Perhaps, the word must be repeated.

Facilitating self-control is an internal rather than an external orientation: as suggested in chapter 4, principals who believe they are internally oriented may believe that they themselves control rather than react to most events and other persons and do not merely react to them; included among the temptations they believe they can control is the *me*, the impulses that spring from within themselves. Two consequences for changes in the degrees of hesitation may be noted. First, persons who already have an internal orientation may be more likely to react positively to plans promoting reflection; and, generally, only principals with certain preexisting proclivities regarding hesitation may respond favorably to change.[60] Second, altering a disposition as basic as orientation undoubtedly cannot be easily achieved and therefore may require a fundamental modification of outlook, perhaps away from invoking fate-destiny doctrines and placing greater emphasis upon determinism. The principal must somehow be convinced that he has the potentiality of controlling himself most of the time and that he is not always at the mercy of

his environment and his own impulses. I can do it, I know
that I can.

> *IN SHORT: yes, indeed, efforts can be made to change
> principals' degrees of hesitation either generally or in specific
> situations; usually the goal is to make them less impulsive,
> infrequently less hesitant or even less reflective; these efforts are
> possible, feasible, but not inevitably successful; obstacles are
> numerous and some moral uncertainty must be overcome.*

Appendix: Survey of Abstracts

The PsycLIT Database contains summaries of the world's literature
in psychology and related disciplines and is compiled from mate-
rial published in Psychological Abstracts and the PsycLIT Database. PsycLIT covers over 1,400 journals in twenty-nine different
languages from approximately fifty-four countries.

The quotation comes from the description of a company
that calls itself "SilverPlatter" and that offers, on a computer terminal, adequate abstracts in English of relevant
studies. For present purposes I secured a printout of the 370
abstracts covering the period between January and September of 1988 that mentioned the word "impulsivity" in the
title or in the abstract itself, regardless of the definition or
the method of measurement. Although I have carefully read
and categorized the abstracts, I would not claim that I have
"content-analyzed" them in a strict sense, which means, in
effect, that the reliability of the categorizations has not been
verified by comparing, for example, my judgments with those
of another person independently reading the same dull materials or a portion of them. In addition, the exact frequency
with which a topic is mentioned I have not indicated: fre-

quency may often be less important than a single study that provides a new or significant insight. For another reason quantification would be misleading since I have here only a sample of abstracts from a single nine-month period. What follows, therefore, are admittedly my impressions of this literature, for which no apology is offered; in each instance, there is in my book at least one footnoted reference to an article that I have read after the abstract thus obtained has called my attention to its existence.

1. *Geographical location.* Almost all of the research has been performed in English-speaking countries, especially the United States and then the United Kingdom. Other contributions come from Western European countries (Norway, Sweden, France, Belgium, Switzerland, and West Germany); there are some too from the U.S.S.R., Yugoslavia, Czechoslovakia, and Romania. Outside of Europe, Israel, India, Japan, the Philippines, and Zambia are represented. The aim of most of these studies seems to have been to investigate impulsivity-reflection in the local setting, but casual and sometimes systematic references are made to Western norms and to the cross-cultural implications of the results.

2. *Interrelations.* Almost every conceivable relationship between impulsivity or reflection and some other variable has been investigated, including fluctuations with the time of day. Attention is paid to drugs, such as amphetamines and benzodiazepines, to discover their effects on the nervous system and behavior or as possible therapeutic agents. Again and again statistical relations are established between hesitancy and other dispositions of the personality that vary from traits to intelligence. Methodological issues are discussed fairly frequently, references are made to problems inherent in the Matching Test, and of course valiant attempts appear that would summarize current or recent research.

3. *Undesirable behavior.* Almost all the behavior with which impulsivity rather than reflection has been associated is considered by all or some investigators to be anti-social or harmful; a partial list in alphabetical order:

abnormality
abusiveness, anger, aggression, violence

addiction to video games
alcoholism
anorexia, bulemia
automobile accidents
avoiding military draft
child molestation
crime
drug addiction
rape
smoking
substance abuse
suicide
truancy
unstable personal or social relations

4. *Handicaps*. Again impulsivity rather than reflection has been found to be associated with:

borderline psychopathologies
brain dysfunction or change
cancer and coronary difficulties
deafness
disabilities
mental disorders or retardation
poisoning
psychopathology
schizophrenia

5. *Psychological problems*. Aside from tendencies toward aphasia and especially hyperactivity, impulsive rather than reflective principals tend to be *deficient* with respect to:

attention
emotional control
learning and memory
reading

reasoning
school subjects
self-control
verbalization

6. *Desirable tendencies.* Few studies directly or indirectly praised impulsivity; those that did found this attribute to have been narrowly adaptive in an experimental situation; to be helpful in playing basketball and in medical training; and to be conducive to flexibility and originality.

7. *Individual and social differences.* Many investigations, though not primarily methodological or theoretical in orientation, have referred to differences among principals without providing an ethical evaluation. Such studies concentrate upon variations with age, gender, place of residence, and spouses.

> *WARNING. These summaries must be cautiously applied to any individual principal or a particular situation. First, with few exceptions they have been based on statistical trends, which means that in each study there is always some overlapping even when the differences between the impulsive and reflective subjects is statistically significant. Then either because different methods or samples of people were employed or simply because human complexity can seldom be reduced to a simple generalization, in some instances contradictory findings have emerged. For example, one study in each case has shown that crime, hyperactivity, and borderline status were not related to the variable of hesitancy. This review of the studies, moreover, necessarily has not conveyed the flavor of the attack upon impulsivity. One sentence from one of the surveys of research among American children must suffice as a sample: in comparison with reflective children, those who are impulsive make "more errors in reading prose when in the primary grades, are more likely to offer incorrect solutions in inductive reasoning problems and visual discrimination tasks, and make more errors of common sense on serial recall tasks."*

Notes

Chapter 1. Clarification

1. Cf. A. T. Welford (1980). Relationships between reaction time and fatigue, stress, age, and sex. In A. T. Welford (ed.), *Reaction times* (pp. 321–354). London: Academic Press.

2. Leonard W. Doob (1988). *Inevitability* (pp. 5–8). Westport, CT: Greenwood Press.

3. Cf. Arthur Kleinman (1980). *Patients and healers in the context of culture.* (chap. 2). Berkeley: University of California.

4. Cf. Michael Ross and Garth J. O. Fletcher (1985). Attribution and social perception. In Gardner Lindzey and Elliot Aronson (eds.), *Handbook of social psychology, 2* (pp. 73–122). New York: Random House.

5. Alan Gewirth (1954). Can man change laws of social science? *Philosophy of Science, 21*, 229–241.

6. Edward Shils (1957). Primordial, personal, sacred, and civil ties. *British Journal of Sociology, 8*, 130–145.

7. Leonard W. Doob (1987). *Slightly beyond skepticism* (pp. 3–4). New Haven: Yale University Press.

8. Cf. Joseph Nuttin (1980), *Motivation et perspectives d'avenir*; Louvain: Presses Universitaires. Joel O. Raynor (1969), Future orientation and motivation of immediate activity, *Psychological Review, 76*, 606–610.

9. Sarnoff A. Mednick (1976), The associative basis of the creative process. In Albert Rothenberg and Carl R. Hausman (eds.), *The creativity question* (pp. 227–237). Durham, NC: Duke University Press.

10. Maurice Loss and Richard W. Wunderlich (1985). A measure of impulsiveness and its relation to extraversion. *Educational and Psychological Measurement, 45,* 251–257.

11. Joseph R. Royce (1973). The conceptual framework of a multifactor theory of individuality. In Joseph R. Royce (ed.), *Multivariate analysis* (pp. 305–407). New York: Academic Press.

12. Without appreciable hesitation I also have an apologetic explanation to offer: through force of habit and through an aversion to prolong sentences, which I am not always able to curb, I am unable to prevent myself most but not all of the time from using the word "he" (including "him" and "his") to refer to a principal in the singular when in fact gender is not the issue. I consider the smarty "s/he" an abomination, as is repeating the noun and substituting "person" or "individual." Sometimes the gender-free "they" does not or cannot be made to emerge gracefully; besides, it is often not desirable and necessary to refer to an or the individual in the same sentence. Perhaps I am influenced by German, the only language besides English in which I think I can easily express myself. In German all nouns have grammatical gender and require masculine, feminine, or neuter pronouns; and the word for "one" is *man*, is genderless, but is pronounced exactly like *Mann* which means "man" in English. Rather than alternating "she" and "he", using "she" in place of "he", or resorting to the plural or "they" when a principal of either gender is the referent, I much prefer to join the battle for women's rights in real life and not through awkward vocabulary.

13. William Kessen and Emil D. Cahan (1986). A century of psychology. *American Scientist, 74,* 640–649.

14. Marvin Zuckerman (ed.) (1983). *Biological bases of sensation seeking, impulsivity, and anxiety.* Hillsdale, NJ: Erlbaum.

15. Philippe Soubrié (1986). Reconciling the role of central serotonin neurons in human and animal behavior. *Behavioral and Brain Sciences, 9,* 319–364.

16. Soubrié, *op. cit.,* pp. 349–355.

17. Cf. Kenneth J. Gergen (1982). *Toward transformation in social knowledge.* New York: Springer-Verlag.

18. Cf. Dariusz Dolinski et al. (1988). Perpetrators' freedom of

choice as a determinant of responsibility attribution. *Journal of Social Psychology, 128,* 441–449.

19. Karl E. Scheibe (1979). *Mirrors, masks, lies, & secrets* (pp. 147–148). New York: Praeger.

20. Karl Zener (1962). Perceptual experience. In Sigmund Koch (ed.), *Psychology, 4* (pp. 516–562). New York: McGraw-Hill.

21. Joseph Nuttin (1984). *Motivation, planning, and action* (p. 213). Hillsdale, NJ: Erlbaum.

Chapter 2. Routes and Measurement

1. Ernest S. Barrett and Jim H. Patton (1983). Impulsivity. In Marvin Zuckerman (ed.), *Biological bases of sensation seeking, impulsivity, and anxiety* (pp. 77–116). Hillsdale, NJ: Erlbaum.

2. Cf. Joachim Tiedemann (1983). Der Kognitive Stil Impulsivität-Reflexivität. *Zeitschrift für Entwicklungspsychologie und Pädagogische Psychologie, 15,* 66–74.

3. E. g., Jerome Kagan (1965). Individual differences in the resolution of response uncertainty. *Journal of Personality and Social Psychology, 2,* 154–160.

4. E. g., Susan W. Barstis and Leroy H. Ford (1977). Reaction-impulsivity, conservation, and the development of ability to control cognitive tempo. *Child Development, 48,* 953–954.

5. E. g., Nathan Kogan (1983). Stylistic variation in childhood and adolescence. In Paul H. Mussen (ed.), *Handbook of child psychology, 3* (pp. 630–706). New York: Wiley.

6. Pedro S. C. Resendiz and Robert Fox (1983). Impulsive *versus* inefficient problem solving in retarded and nonretarded Mexican children. *Journal of Psychology, 114,* 187–191.

7. Tullio D. Pitassi and Stuard I. Offenbach (1978). Delay of reinforcement effects with reflective and impulsive children. *Journal of Genetic Psychology, 133,* 3–8. Cf. Stanley B. Messer (1976). Reaction and impulsivity. *Psychological Bulletin, 83,* 1026–1053.

8. James B. Victor et al. (1985). Relations between reflection-impulsivity and behavioral impulsivity in preschool children. *Developmental Psychology, 21,* 141–148.

9. J. Holzi (1983). Der Einfluss des Impulsivität auf das Lösen von Analogieaufgaben. *Zeitschrift für Psychologie, 191,* 271–281.

10. Cf. Pedro Solís-Cámera R. and Pedro Solís-Cámera V. (1987). Is the matching familiar figures test a measure of cognitive style? *Perceptual & Motor Skills, 64,* 59–74.

11. Jerome Kagan (1966). Reflection-impulsivity. *Journal of Abnormal Psychology, 71*, 17–24.

12. Diana M. Drake (1970). Perceptual correlates of impulsive and reflective behavior. *Developmental Psychology, 2*, 202–214. Cf. Tamar Zelniker et al. (1972). Analysis and modification of search strategies of impulsive and reflective children in the matching familiar figures test. *Child Development, 43*, 321–335.

13. Elias Duryea and John A. Glover (1982). A review of the research on reflection and impulsivity in children. *Genetic Psychology Monographs, 106*, 217–237.

14. Victor, op. cit.

15. Howard Margolis et al. (1980). The validity of form F of the matching familiar figures test with kindergarten children. *Journal of Experimental Child Psychology, 29*, 12–22.

16. Scott J. Dickman (1988). Impulsivity and speed accuracy tradeoffs in information processing. *Journal of Personality and Social Psychology, 54*, 279–290.

17. Bill Jones and Jim Duffy (1982). An analysis of performance by pre-school children on the *KRISP* and on a length discrimination task. *Acta Psychologica, 52*, 197–211.

18. Peter Oas (1984). Validity of the draw-a-person and Bender Gestalt tests as measures of impulsivity with adolescents. *Journal of Consulting and Clinical Psychology, 52*, 1011–1019.

19. Aron W. Siegman (1961). The relationship between time perspective, time estimation, and impulse control in a group of young offenders and in a control group. *Journal of Consulting Psychology, 25*, 470–475.

20. Kenneth Purcell (1965). The thematic apperception test and anti-social behavior. In Bernard I. Murstein (ed.), *Handbook of projective techniques* (pp. 547–560). New York: Basic Books.

21. S. B. G. Eysenck and H. J. Eysenck (1977). The place of impulsiveness in a dimensional system of personality. *British Journal of Social and Clinical Psychology, 16*, 57–68.

22. Ernest S. Barratt (1965). Factor analysis of some psychometric measures of impulsiveness and anxiety. *Psychological Reports, 16*, 547–554.

23. Daisy Schalling et al. (1983). Impulsive cognitive style and inability to tolerate boredom. In Zuckerman (ed.), op. cit. (pp. 123–145).

24. Richard L. Schanck (1932). A study of community and its groups and institutions conceived of as behavior of individuals. *Psychological Monograph, 43*, n. 2.

25. Jim Stevenson and Jane Fielding (1985). Ratings of temperament in families of young twins. *British Journal of Developmental Psychology*, *3*, 143–152.

26. John Jung (1987). Anticipating excuses in relation to expected versus actual task performance. *Journal of Psychology*, *121*, 413–421.

27. Cf. Shelly Chaiken and Charles Stangor (1987). Attitudes and attitude change. *Annual Review of Psychology*, *38*, 575–630.

28. Cf. D. S. Moskowitz (1986). Comparison of self-reports, reports by knowledgeable informants, and behavioral observation data. *Journal of Personality*, *54*, 294–317.

29. David W. Gerbing et al. (1987). Toward a conceptualization of impulsivity. *Multivariate Behavioral Research*, *22*, 357–379.

30. Robert A. Prentky and Raymond A. Knight (1986). Impulsivity in the lifestyle and criminal behavior of sexual offenders. *Criminal Justice and Behavior*, *13*, 141–164.

31. David Shapiro (1965). *Neurotic styles* (pp. 134–135). New York: Basic Books.

32. Alex Tarnopolsky and Mark Berelowitz (1984). "Borderline personality." *British Journal of Psychiatry*, *144*, 364–369. Cf. Robert M. Mowbray (1972). In Brian Davies et al. (eds.), *Depressive illness* (pp. 278–398). Springfield: Charles C. Thomas.

33. Peter Oas (1983). Impulsive behavior and assessment of impulsivity with hospitalized adolescents. *Psychological Reports*, *53*, 764–766.

34. William M. Reynolds and Kevin D. Stark (1986). Self-control in children. *Journal of Abnormal Child Psychology*, *14*, 13–23.

Chapter 3. Culture and Society

1. Clifford Geertz (1973). *The interpretation of cultures* (p. 49). New York: Basic Books.

2. Udaz Jain and Suraj Mal (1984). Effect of prolonged deprivation on attribution of causes of success and failure. *Journal of Social Psychology*, *124*, 143–149.

3. William Shakespeare. *As you like it* (act 2, scene 7).

4. Kurt Lewin (1948). *Resolving social conflicts* (pp. 9–10). New York: Harpers.

5. E. E. Maccoby (1984). Socialization and developmental change. *Child Development*, *55*, 317–328.

6. Cf. Elias Duryear and John A. Glover (1982). A review of the

research on reflection and impulsivity. *Genetic Psychology Monographs, 106,* 217–237.

7. Duane G. Ollendick and Brenda J. Otto (1984). MMPI characteristics of parents referred for child-custody studies. *Journal of Psychology, 117,* 227–232.

8. Susan S. Davis (1983). *Patience and power* (pp. 37, 43). Cambridge, MA: Schenkman.

9. Richard Lynn (1981). Cross-cultural differences in neuroticism, extraversion, and psychotism. In Richard Lynn (ed.), *Dimensions of personality* (pp. 263–313). Oxford: Pergamon.

10. Lesley Clark and Gaeme S. Hulford (1983). Does cognitive style account for cultural differences in scholastic achievement? *Journal of Cross-Cultural Psychology, 14,* 279–296.

11. Pedro Solís-Cámara R. et al. (1985). Children's human figure drawings and impulsive style at two levels of socioeconomic status. *Perceptual and Motor Skills, 61,* 1039–1048.

12. Pedro Solís-Cámara R. and Pedro Solís-Cámara V. (1987). Is the matching familiar figures test a measure of cognitive style? *Perceptual and Motor Skills, 64,* 59–74.

13. Oliver Cox (1959). *Caste, class, and race* (p. 401). New York: Monthly Review Press.

14. Cf. John W. M. Whiting and Irvin L. Child (1953). *Child training and personality.* New Haven: Yale University Press.

15. Louis H. Stewart (1977). Birth order and political leadership. In Margaret G. Hermann (ed.), *A psychological examination of political leaders* (pp. 205–236). New York: Free Press.

16. Larry Gates et al. (1988). Birth order and its relationship to depression, anxiety, and self-concept test scores in children. *Journal of Genetic Psychology, 149,* 29–34.

17. R. B. Zajonc et al. (1979). The birth order puzzle. *Journal of Personality and Social Psychology, 37,* 1325–1341.

18. Felicia C. Goldstein and Howard A. Rollings (1983). Maternal teaching styles, children's response patterns, and mother-child reflection-impulsivity. *Journal of Genetic Psychology, 142,* 315–316.

19. Karen K. Dion (1985). Socialization in adulthood. In Gardner Lindzey and Elliot Aronson (eds.), *Handbook of social psychology, 2,* 123–147. New York: Random House.

20. Cf. Richard E. Tremblay et al. (1984). Le développement cognif des préadolescents. *Bulletin de Psychologie, 38,* 13–22.

21. Thomas Davey (1987). *A generation divided* (p. 125). Durham, NC: Duke University Press.

NOTES

22. Harry Fowler (1965). *Curiosity and exploratory behavior* (pp. 25, 30; italics omitted). New York: Macmillan.

23. Kazuo Yamaguchi and Denise B. Kandel (1985). Dynamic relationships between premarital cohabitation. *American Sociological Review, 50,* 530–546.

24. Cf. Robert S. Weiss (1975). *Marital separation* (pp. 44–46). New York: Basic Books.

25. Cf. Christopher R. Stones (1986). Love styles revisited. *Human Relations, 39,* 379–382.

26. Cited by Walter Mischel (1984). Convergencies and challenges in the search for consistency. *American Psychologist, 39,* 351–364.

27. D. R. Davies and R. Paràsuraman (1981). *The psychology of vigilance* (p. 22). London: Academic Press.

28. Leonard W. Doob (1967). Scales for assaying psychological modernization in Africa. *Public Opinion Quarterly, 31,* 414–421. Cf. Harrison G. Gough (1976), A measure of individual modernity; *Journal of Personality Assessment, 40,* 3–9.

29. Gregg C. Oden (1987). Concept, knowledge, and thought. *Annual Review of Psychology, 38,* 203–227.

30. Cf. Herbert H. Clark (1985). Language use and language users. In Lindzey and Aronson, op. cit. 2 (pp. 179–231).

31. Maria Tatar (1987). *The hard facts of the Grimms' fairy tales* (p. 72). Princeton: Princeton University Press.

32. J. Svennung (1958). Anredeformen. *Kungl. Humanistiska Vetenskapssamfundet I Uppsala, 42.*

33. Cf. Leonard W. Doob (1961). *Communication in Africa* (chap. 2). New Haven: Yale University Press.

34. Gordon W. Allport and Henry S. Odbert (1936). Trait-names, a psycho-lexical study. *Psychological Monograph, 47,* n. 211.

35. Leonard W. Doob (1960). The effect of codability upon the afferent and efferent functioning of language. *Journal of Social Psychology, 52,* 3–15.

36. Howard Gardner et al. (1978). The development of figurative language. In Kent T. Nelson (ed.), *Children's language* (pp. 1–38). New York: Gardner Press.

37. Cf. H. Paul Grice (1975). Logic and conversation. In Donald Davidson and Gilbert Harmon (eds.), *The logic of grammar* (pp. 64–75). Encino, CA: Dickenson.

38. Christine Brooke-Rose (1965). *A grammar of metaphor* (pp. 23–24). London: Secker & Warburg.

39. Howard R. Pollio (1974). *The psychology of symbolic activity* (p. 77). Reading, MA: Addison-Wesley.

40. Allan Paivio (1979). Psychological processes in the comprehension of metaphor. In Andrew Ortony (ed.), *Metaphor and thought* (pp. 150–171). Cambridge, UK: Cambridge University Press.

41. E. g., Earl R. Mac Cormac (1985). *A cognitive theory of metaphor* (pp. 58–59). Cambridge, MA: MIT Press.

42. Roger Brown (1958). *Words and things* (p. 142). New York: Free Press. Cf. Geertz, op. cit. (p. 45).

43. Gardner, op. cit. (pp. 12–13).

44. Kenneth J. Gergen (1982). *Toward transformation in social knowledge* (p. 79). New York: Springer-Verlag.

45. Hans Kreitler and Shulamith Kreitler (1976). *Cognitive orientation and behavior* (pp. 25–28). New York: Springer-Verlag.

46. Marie Jahoda (1982). *Employment and unemployment* (pp. 83–84). London: Cambridge University Press.

47. Cf. Dane Archer (1985). Social deviance. In Lindzey and Aronson (eds.), op. cit. *2* (743–804).

48. Wolfgang Köhler (1938). *The place of values in a world of facts* (p. 186). New York: Liveright.

49. Cf. Lawrence E. Marks et al. (1987). Perceiving similarity and comprehending metaphor. *Monographs for the Society for Research in Child Development, 52*, no. 1.

50. Cited by Howard R. Pollio and Michael K. Smith (1980). Metaphoric competence and complex human problem solving. In Richard P. Honeck and Robert Hoffman (eds.), *Cognition and figurative language* (pp. 365–392). Hillsdale, NJ: Erlbaum.

51. Kathleen Connor and Nathan Kogan (1980). Topic-vehicle relations in metaphor. In Honeck and Hoffman (eds.), op. cit. (pp. 283–308).

52. Pollio and Smith, op. cit. Cf. Nathan Kogan (1983). Stylistic variation in childhood and adolescence. In Paul H. Mussen (ed.), *Handbook of child psychology* (pp. 630–706). New York: Wiley.

53. Bruce B. Henderson et al. (1985). Children's exploratory behavior and the generalization of a prohibition. *Journal of Genetic Psychology, 146*, 37–64.

54. Cf. Geertz, op. cit. (pp. 22).

55. Peter A. Andersen and Jane F. Andersen. (1984). The exchange of nonverbal intimacy. *Journal of Nonverbal Behavior, 8*, 327–347.

56. Robert B. Textor (1967). *A cross-cultural summary* (category 77). New Haven: HRAF Press.

57. Doob. *Communication in Africa*, op. cit. (pp. 243–244).
58. Cf. Joseph Berger (1988). Price of illiteracy translates into poverty and humiliation. *New York Times*, September 6, 1988; A1 and B8.

Chapter 4. Personality

1. Robert W. White (1959). Motivation reconsidered. *Psychological Review, 66*, 297–333.
2. Michael Davis (1986). Pharmacological and anatomical analysis of fear conditioning using the fear-potential startle paradigm. *Behavioral Neuroscience, 100*, 814–824. Howard S. Hoffman and James R. Ison (1980). Reflex modification in the domain of startle. *Psychological Review, 87*, 175–189.
3. Cf. George Mahl (1956). Disturbances and silences in the patient's speech in psychopathology. *Journal of Abnormal and Social Psychology, 53*, 1–15.
4. Gerd Quinting (1971). *Hesitation phenomena in adult aphasic and normal speech* (pp. 56–57). Hague: Mouton.
5. Cf. Howard Maclay and Charles E. Osgood (1959). Hesitation phenomena in spontaneous English speech. *Word, 15*, 19–44.
6. William S. Foster (1915). On the perseveration tendency. *American Journal of Psychology, 25*, 393–426.
7. Cf. Rosa P. Abelló et al. (1986). Consensus and contrast components in landscape preference. *Environment and Behavior, 18*, 155–178.
8. Cited by Karen Kennerly (1973). *Hesitant wolf and scrupulous fox* (p. 52). New York: Random House.
9. David M. Brodzinsky (1975). The role of conceptual tempo in children's humor development. *Developmental Psychology, 11*, 843–850.
10. Edward H. Sewell (1984). Appreciation of cartoons with profanity in captions. *Psychological Reports, 54*, 583–587.
11. D. K. B. Nias (1981). Humour and personality. In Richard Lynn (ed.), *Dimensions of personality* (pp. 287–313). Oxford: Pergamon.
12. Paul Ekman and Harriet Oster (1979). Facial expressions of emotion. *Annual Review of Psychology, 30*, 527–554.
13. Michael Polanyi (1967). *The tacit dimension* (pp. 4, 5; italics deleted). Garden City: Doubleday. Cf. James J. Gibson and Anne D. Pick (1963). Prediction of another person's looking behavior. *American Journal of Psychology, 76*, 386–394.

14. Cf. Stephen Nowicki and Mark Hartigan (1988). Accuracy of facial affect recognition as a function of locus of control orientation and anticipated interpersonal interaction. *Journal of Social Psychology, 128*, 363–372.

15. Claire Tremblay et al. (1987). The recognition of adults' and children's facial expressions of emotions. *Journal of Psychology, 121*, 341–350.

16. Polanyi, op. cit. (pp. 6, 35).

17. Cf. Ekman and Oster, op. cit.

18. Bennett B. Murdock (1974). *Human memory* (p. 178). Potomac, MD: Erlbaum.

19. Cf. Robert P. Abelson (1976); Script processing attitude formation and decision making. In John S. Carroll and John W. Payne (eds.), *Cognition and social behavior* (pp. 33–45). Hillsdale, NJ: Erlbaum. Elizabeth P. Lorch and Donna G. Horn (1986). Habituation of attention to irrelevant stimuli in elementary school children. *Journal of Experimental Child Psychology, 41*. 184–197

20. Betty Ann Levy and John Begin (1984). Proofreading familiar text. *Memory & Cognition, 12*, 621–632.

21. Dennis Krebs and Dale T. Miller (1985). Altruism and aggression. In Gardner Lindzey and Elliot Aronson (eds.), *Handbook of social psychology, 2* (pp. 1–71). New York: Random House. Cf. John H. Harvey and Gifford Weary (1981). *Perspectives on attributional processes* (chap. 1). Dubuque: W. C. Brown.

22. Hans J. Eysenck and Michael W. Eysenck (1985). *Personality and individual differences*. New York: Plenum Press.

23. *Idem.*, pp. 69–70.

24. Marvin Zuckerman (ed.) (1983). *Biological bases of sensation seeking, impulsivity, and anxiety* (p. 249). Hillsdale, NJ: Erlbaum.

25. J. G. O'Gorman and Jacqueline E. Lloyd (1987). Extraversion, impulsiveness, and EEG alpha activity. *Personality and Individual Differences, 8*, 169–174.

26. Sandra Scarr (1966). Genetic factors in activity motivation. *Child Development, 37*, 663–673.

27. H. J. Eysenck (1983). A biometrical-genetical analysis of impulsive and sensation seeking behavior. In Zuckerman, op. cit. (pp. 1–36).

28. Zuckerman (1983). Comments. In Zuckerman, op. cit. (pp. 29–30).

29. Eysenck and Eysenck (1985), op. cit. (pp. 69, 74, 355).

30. Regina M. Yondo and Jerome Kagan (1970). The effect of

task complexity on reflection-impulsivity. *Cognitive Psychology, 1,* 192–200.

31. Jerome Kagan (1965). Impulsivity and reading ability in primary grade children. *Child Development, 36,* 609–629. Jerome Kagan et al. (1966). Modifiability of an impulsive tempo. *Journal of Educational Psychology, 57,* 359–365.

32. Jerome Kagan et al. (1966). Conceptual impulsivity and inductive reasoning. *Child Development, 37,* 583–594.

33. Jerome Kagan (1971). *Understanding children* (p. 128). New York: Harcourt Brace Jovanovich.

34. Jerome Kagan (1965). Individual differences in the resolution of response uncertainty. *Journal of Personality and Social Psychology, 2,* 154–160. Kagan (1966). Reflection-impulsivity. *Journal of Abnormal Psychology, 71,* 17–24.

35. Jerome Kagan (1979). *A cross-cultural study of cognitive development* (p. 75). Chicago: University of Chicago Press.

36. Jerome Kagan (1984). *The nature of the child* (p. 228). New York: Basic Books.

37. Howard Margolis et al. (1980). The validity of form F of the matching familiar figures test with kindergarten children. *Journal of Experimental Child Psychology, 29,* 12–22.

38. Harry A. Murray et al. (1938). *Explorations in personality* (pp. 205–206, 508–512). New York: Oxford University Press.

39. Douglas N. Jackson (1967). *Personality research form manual* (pp. 6, 7, 48). Goshen, NY: Research Psychologists Press.

40. OSS Assessment Staff (1948). *Assessment of men.* New York: Rinehart.

41. Ann Howard and Douglas W. Bray (1988). *Managerial lives in transition.* New York: Guilford.

42. Arnold H. Buss and Robert Plomin (1975). *A temperamental theory of personality development* (pp. 5, 8, 17, 122–147, 187). New York: Wiley.

43. Calvin S. Hall and Robert L. Van de Castle (1966). *The content analysis of dreams* (pp. 158–194). New York: Appleton-Century-Crofts.

44. Cf. Seymour Epstein and Edward J. O'Brien (1985). The person-situation debate in historical and current perspective. *Psychological Bulletin, 98,* 513–537.

45. David Raden (1985). Strength-related attitude dimensions. *Social Psychology Quarterly, 48,* 312–330.

46. Thelma E. Lobel et al. (1985). Guilt feelings and locus of

control of concentration camp survivors. *International Journal of Social Psychology, 31,* 170–175.

47. E. g. Ernest S. Barratt (1983). The biological bases of impulsiveness. *Personality & Individual Differences, 4,* 387–391. Stanley B. Messer (1976). Reaction and impulsivity. *Psychological Bulletin, 83,* 1026–1053. Frantisek Sebej et al. (1984). The relation of subjective and physiological correlates of anger and some cognitive and personality traits. *Studia Psychologica, 26,* 93–103.

48. R. De V. Peters and Gary A. Bernfeld (1983). Reflection-impulsivity and social reasoning. *Developmental Psychology, 19,* 78–81.

49. Mark A. Barnett and Vera McMinimy (1988). Influence of the reasons for the other's affect on preschoolers' empathic response. *Journal of Genetic Psychology, 149,* 153–162.

50. Marvin Zuckerman (1979). *Sensation seeking* (pp. 107–109; chaps. 6–8). Hillsdale, NJ: Erlbaum.

51. Milton Rokeach (1960). *The open and closed mind* (p. 57). New York: Basic Books.

52. James C. Crumbaugh and Leonard T. Maholick (1964). An experimental study in existentialism. *Journal of Clinical Psychology, 20,* 200–207. Crumbaugh (1968). Cross-validation of purpose-in-life test based on Frankl's concepts. *Journal of Individual Psychology, 24,* 74–81.

53. Joyce Hickson (1985). Psychological research on empathy. *Psychological Reports, 57,* 91–94. Rafael Moses (1985). Empathy and dis-empathy in political conflict. *Political Psychology, 6,* 135–139.

54. Albert Mehrabian and Norman Epstein (1972). A measure of emotional empathy. *Journal of Personality, 40,* 525–543.

55. Mirja Kalliopuska (1984). Empathy in children and social class. *Psychological Reports, 55,* 132–134.

56. Bruce E. Chlopan et al. (1985). Empathy. *Journal of Personality and Social Psychology, 48,* 635–653.

57. Davis C. Glass and Charles S. Carver (1980). Helplessness and coronary-prone personality. In Judy Garber and Martin E. P. Seligman, *Human helplessness* (pp. 223–243). New York: Academic Press.

58. Peter Seraganian (1985). Behavioural aspects of coronary heart disease. *Canadian Psychology, 26,* 113–120. Thomas L. Tang (1988). Effects of type A personality and leisure ethic on Chinese college students' leisure activities and academic performance. *Journal of Social Psychology, 128,* 153–158.

59. Julia B. Rotter (1966). Generalized expectancies for internal versus external control of reinforcement. *Psychological Monographs*, *80*, no. 609.

60. Messer, op. cit. Cf. Michael D. Berzonsky (1974). Reflectivity, internality, and animistic thinking. *Child Development*, *45*, 785–789.

61. Leonard W. Doob (1988). *Inevitability* (p. 24). Westport, CT: Greenwood Press.

62. Michael Frese et al. (1987). Goal orientation and planfulness. *Journal of Personality and Social Psychology*, *52*, 1182–1194.

63. Laura P. Otis (1984). Factors influencing the willingness to taste unusual foods. *Psychological Reports*, *54*, 739–745.

64. Leonard W. Doob (1971). *Patterning of time* (chap. 2). New Haven: Yale University Press.

65. Ernest S. Barratt (1981). Time perception, cortical evoked potentials, and impulsiveness. In J. Ray et al. (eds.), *Violence and the violent individual* (pp. 87–95). Jamaica, NY: Spectrum. Barratt and Jim H. Patton (1983). Cognitive, behavioral and psychophysiological correlates. In Zuckerman (1983), op. cit. (pp. 77–116).

66. Messer, op. cit. (p. 1034).

67. Thomas Achenbach (1969). Cue learning, assoiative responding, and school performance in children. *Developmental Psychology*, *1*, 717–725.

68. Nathan Kogan (1983). Stylistic variation in childhood and adolescence. In Paul H. Mussen (ed.), *Handbook of child psychology*, *3*, (pp. 630–706). New York: Wiley.

69. Ed Cairns (1978). Age and conceptual tempo. *Journal of Genetic Psychology*, *133*, 13–17.

70. Stanley B. Messer and David M. Brodzinsky (1981). Three-year stability of reflection-impulsivity in young adolescents. *Developmental Psychology*, *17*, 848–850.

71. Per F. Gjerde et al. (1985). Longitudinal consistency of matching familiar figures test performance from early childhood to preadolescence. *Developmental Psychology*, *21*, 262–271.

72. Sybil Eysenck et al. (1984). Age norms for impulsiveness, venturesomeness, and empathy. *Personality & Individual Differences*, *5*, 315–321.

73. Daisy Schalling et al. (1983). Impulsive cognitive style and inability to tolerate boredom. In Zuckerman (1983), op. cit. (pp. 123–145).

74. Robert Kail (1986). Sources of age differences in speed of processing. *Developmental Psychology*, *57*, 969–987.

75. Neil J. Salkind et al. (1978). Cognitive tempo in American, Japanese, and Israeli children. *Child Development, 49,* 1025–1027.

76. Cf. Claude Steele et al. (1986). Drinking your troubles away. *Journal of Abnormal Psychology, 95,* 173–180.

77. Cf. Mark H. Waugh (1984). A temperamental and developmental model for personality assessment. *Personality & Individual Differences, 5,* 355–358.

78. William J. McGuire (1984). Search for the self. In Robert Zurcher et al. (eds.), *Personality and the prediction of behavior* (pp. 73–120). Orlando: Academic Press.

79. Cf. E. Torry Higgins et al. (1982). Individual construct accessibility and subjective impressions and recall. *Journal of Personality and Social Psychology, 43,* 35–47. Hazel Markus and Paula Nurius (1986). Possible selves. *American Psychologist, 41,* 954–969.

80. Susan M. Anderson and Lee Ross (1984). Self-knowledge and social inference. *Journal of Personality and Social Psychology, 46,* 280–293.

81. Morris M. Haynes et al. (1988). Differences in self-concept among high, average, and low achieving high school sophomores. *Journal of Social Psychology, 128,* 259–264.

82. Margaret Westway and M. Skuy (1984). Self-esteem and the educational and vocational aspirations of adolescent girls in South Africa. *South African Journal of Psychology, 14,* 113–117.

83. Alan Richardson (1984). *The experiential dimension of psychology* (p. 83). St Lucia, Australia: University of Queensland Press.

84. Cf. Harry T. Reis and Laurie B. Burns (1982). The salience of the self in response to inequity. *Journal of Experimental Social Psychology, 18,* 464–475.

85. Cf. C. R. Synder et al. (1985). On the self-serving function of social anxiety. *Journal of Personality and Social Psychology, 48,* 970–980.

86. Cf. Ronald B. Marolis and Clifford R. Mynatt (1986). The effects of external and self-administered reward on high base rate behavior. *Cognitive Theory and Research, 10,* 109–122.

87. Richard D. Lennox and Raymond W. Wolfe (1984). Revision of the self-monitoring test. *Journal of Personality and Social Psychology, 46,* 1349–1364.

88. Hazel Markus and Elissa Wurf (1987). The dynamic self-concept. *Annual Review of Psychology, 38,* 299–337.

89. Cf. William McGuire (1985). Attitudes and attitude change. In Lindzey and Aronson, op. cit. *2* (pp. 233–346). Robert S. Wyer (1974). Some implications of the "Socratic effect" for alternative models of cognitive consistency. *Journal of Personality, 42,* 399–419.

90. I. Howard Marshall (1969). *Kept by the power of God* (pp. 50, 58, 206–208). London: Epworth Press.

91. Judith Rodin (1985). The application of social psychology. In Lindzey and Aronson, op. cit. 2 (pp. 805–881).

92. Cf. David Y. Ho (1976). On the concept of face. *American Journal of Sociology, 81*, 867–884.

93. Adrian Furnham et al. (1985). Type A behavior pattern and attribution of responsibility. *Motivation and Emotion, 9*, 39–51.

94. Kirk R. Blankstein and Janet Polivy (1982). Emotion, self-control, and self-modification. In Kirk R. Blankstein and Janet Polivy (eds.), *Self-control and self-modification* (pp. 1–27). New York: Plenum.

95. Richard V. Ericson et al. (1987). *Visualizing deviance* (pp. 352–356). Toronto: University of Toronto Press.

96. George Gerbner et al. (1980). *Violence profile*. Philadelphia: Annenberg School of Communications.

97. Buss and Plomin, op. cit. (p. 203).

98. R. J. Madigan and A. K. Bollenbach (1986). The effects of induced mood on irrational thoughts and views of the world. *Cognitive Therapy and Research, 10*, 547–562.

99. Bill S. Moore et al. (1973). Affect and altruism. *Developmental Psychology, 8*, 99–104.

100. R. F. S. Job (1987). The effect of mood on helping behavior. *Journal of Social Psychology, 127*, 323–328.

101. Cf. Gordon H. Bower (1981). Mood and memory. *American Psychologist, 36*, 129–148. Jerome L. Singer and John Kolligian (1987). Personality. *Annual Review of Psychology, 38*, 533–574.

102. David F. Dinges et al. (1985). Assessing performance upon abrupt awakening from naps during quasi-continuous operations. *Behavior Research Methods, Instruments, and Computers, 17*, 37–45.

103. Michael F. Pignatiello (1986). Musical mood induction. *Journal of Abnormal Psychology, 95*, 295–297.

104. Judson Mills (1965). The effect of certainty on exposure to information prior to commitment. *Journal of Experimental Psychology, 1*, 348–355.

Chapter 5. Other Persons

1. Mark Snyder (1974). The self-monitoring of expressive behavior. *Journal of Personality and Social Psychology, 30*, 526–537.

2. Stephen R. Briggs et al. (1980). An analysis of the self-monitoring scale. *Journal of Personality and Social Psychology, 38*, 679–686.

3. Harold H. Kelley (1968). Two functions of reference groups. In Herbert H. Hyman and Eleanor Singer (eds.), *Readings in reference group theory and research* (pp. 77–83). New York: Free Press.

4. Ans E. M. Appelgryn and Johan M. Nieuwoudt (1988). Relative deprivation and the ethnic attitudes of blacks and Afrikaans-speaking whites in South Africa. *Journal of Social Psychology, 128,* 311–323.

5. Cf. Lee Ross (1977). The intuitive psychologist and his shortcomings. In Leonard Berkowitz (ed.), *Advances in experimental social psychology, 10,* (pp. 173–220). New York: Academic Press.

6. Herbert Blumer (1969). *Symbolic interactionism* (p. 12). Englewood Cliffs, NJ: Prentice-Hall.

7. Cf. Ralph Juhnke et al. (1987). Effects of attractiveness and nature of request on helping behavior. *Journal of Social Psychology, 127,* 317–322.

8. E. Tory Higgins and John A. Bargh (1987). Social cognition and social perception. *Annual Review of Psychology, 38,* 369–425.

9. Cf. William J. McGuire (1984). Search for the self. In Robert A. Zurcher et al. (eds.), *Personality and the prediction of behavior* (pp. 73–120). Orlando: Academic Press.

10. Cf. Mark Snyder (1984). When belief creates reality. *Advances in Experimental Social Psychology, 18,* 247–305.

11. Floyd H. Allport (1924). *Social psychology* (pp. 305–307). Boston: Houghton Mifflin.

12. Cf. Edward T. Hall (1966). *The hidden dimension.* Garden City: Doubleday.

13. George Banziger and Renée Simmons (1984). Emotion, attractiveness, and interpersonal space. *Journal of Social Psychology, 124,* 255–256.

14. Julian B. Rotter (1981). The psychological situation in social-learning theory. In David Magnusson (ed.), *Toward a psychology of situations* (pp. 169–178). Hillsdale, NJ: Erlbaum.

15. Cf. David Watson (1982). The actor and the observed. *Psychological Bulletin, 92,* 682–700. Gifford Weary (1979). Self-serving attributional biases. *Journal of Personality and Social Psychology, 38,* 1419–1420.

16. Cf. Timothy M. Osberg and J. Sidney Shrauger (1986). Retrospective versus prospective causal judgments of self and others. *Journal of Personality and Social Psychology, 126,* 169–178.

17. Mark Snyder (1984). When belief creates reality. *Advances in Experimental Social Psychology, 18,* 247–305.

18. Hyunjung Bae and Kathleen S. Crittended (1989). From at-

tributions to dispositional inferences. *Journal of Social Psychology*, *129*, 481–489.

19. Jerald Jellison and Robert Arkin (1977). Social comparison of abilities. In Jerry M. Suls and Richard L. Miller (eds.), *Social comparison processes* (pp. 235–257). New York: Wiley. Wyndol Furman and Karen L. Bierman (1984). Children's conceptions of friendship. *Developmental Psychology*, *20*, 925–931.

20. Esther R. Fein (1988). Veterans from 2 armies and 2 wars finding shared wounds in Moscow. *New York Times*, 3 October 1988, A12.

21. Cf. Elie Kedourie (1987). "One-man-one-vote." *South Africa International*, *18*, no. 1, 1–4.

22. George Bach-y-Rita et al. (1971) Episodic dyscontrol. *American Journal of Psychiatry*, *127*, 1473–1478.

23. Thomas L. Wright et al. (1985). Satisfaction and things not said. *Small Group Behavior*, *16*, 565–572.

24. Fatima Meer (1987). The trial of Andrew Zondo. (pp. 45–46, 109–110, 116–117, 145). Johannesburg: Skotavile.

25. Thomas L. Morrison et al. (1984). Member perceptions in small and large Tavistock groups. *Journal of Social Psychology*, *124*, 209–217.

26. Karl E. Scheibe (1979). *Mirrors, masks, lies, and secrets* (p. 5). New York: Praeger.

27. Herbert C. Kelman and V. Lee Hamilton (1989). *Crimes of obedience* (pp. 158–162). New Haven: Yale University Press.

28. Ernest R. Hilgard (1965). *Hypnotic susceptibility* (pp. 21, 49, 180–181, 194–195, 394). New York: Harcourt Brace Jovanovich.

29. Charles F. Bond and Linda J. Titus (1983). Social facilitation. *Psychological Bulletin*, *94*, 265–292.

30. Cf. Rustemli Ahmet (1988). The effects of personal space invasion on impressions and decisions. *Journal of Psychology*, *122*, 113–118.

31. Kurt Lewin (1948). *Resolving social conflict* (p. 23). New York: Harpers. Paul A. Bell et al. (1988). Friendship and freedom of movement as moderators of sex differences in interpersonal distancing. *Journal of Social Psychology*, *128*, 305–310.

32. Cf. Fred J. Van Staden (1984). Developments in defining the experience of crowding. *South African Journal of Psychology*, *14*, 20–22.

33. J. J. Pia et al. (1966). *Beginning in Somali* (p. 7). Syracuse, NY: Syracuse University Press.

34. G. Terence Wilson (1982). Alcohol and anxiety. In Kirk R.

Blankstein and Janet Polivy (eds.), *Self-control and self-modification* (pp. 117–141). New York: Plenum.

35. Thomas D. Cook et al. (1977). The construct validity of relative deprivation. In Jerry M. Suls and Richard L. Miller, *Social comparison processes* (pp. 307–333). New York: Wiley.

36. Saul M. Kassin (1984). TV cameras, public self consciousness, and mock jury performance. *Journal of Experimental Social Psychology, 20*, 336–349.

37. Bernard P. Dauenhauer (1980). *Silence* (pp. 109–112). Bloomington: Indiana University Press.

38. Max Picard (1952). *The world of silence* (pp. 85, 95, 205, 221). South Bend: Regnery/Gateway.

39. Charles Courtenay (1916). *The empire of silence* (pp. 18, 221, 290). London: Sampson Low, Marston.

40. Letitia A. Peplau and Daniel Perlman. *Loneliness* (especially part 1 and chap. 7). New York: Wiley.

41. Picard, *op. cit.* (p. 29).

42. Dan Russell et al. (1980). The revised UCLA loneliness scale. *Journal of Personality and Social Psychology, 39*, 472–480.

43. Huguette Hirsig (1979). *Solitude* (p. 106). Montreal: Stanké.

44. Robert Sayre (1978). *Solitude in society* (especially pp. 195–199). Cambridge, MA: Harvard University Press.

45. Marcel Eck (1970). *Lies and truth* (pp. 1 et seq.). New York: Macmillan.

46. Cf. Ellen Berscheid (1985). Interpersonal attraction. In Gardner Lindzey and Elliot Aronson (eds.), *Handbook of social psychology, 2* (pp. 413–484). New York: Random House.

47. Eck, *op. cit.* (pp. 29, 81).

48. Richard A. Dwyer and Richard E. Langenfelter (1984). *Lying on the eastern slope* (p. 50). Miami: University Presses of Florida.

49. Fred E. Inbau (1948). *Lie detection and criminal interrogation* (especially pp. 1, 5, 30, 67). Baltimore: William & Wilkins. Paul Ekman (1985). *Telling lies* (chap. 7). New York: Norton.

Chapter 6. Situations

1. George Mahl (1956). Disturbances and silences in patients' speech pathology. *Journal of Abnormal and Social Psychology, 53*, 1–15.

2. Stephen B. Knouse (1989). The role of attribution theory in personnel employment selection. *Journal of General Psychology, 116*, 183–196.

3. Vernon H. Mark and Frank R. Ervin (1970). *Violence and the brain* (pp. 97–108, 142–143). New York: Harper & Row.

4. Cf. David Magnusson (ed.) (1981). *Toward a psychology of situations*. Hillsdale, NJ: Erlbaum. Walter Mischel (1984). On the predictability of behavior and the structure of personality. In Robert A. Zucker et al. (eds.), *Personality and the prediction of behavior* (pp. 269–305). Orlando: Academic Press. E. Tory Higgins and John A. Bargh (1987). Social cognition and social perception. *Annual Review of Psychology, 38*, 369–425.

5. Daryl J. Bem and David C. Funder (1978). Predicting more of the people more of the time. *Psychological Review, 85*, 485–501. Julian B. Rotter (1981). The psychological situation in social-learning theory. In Magnusson, op. cit. (pp. 169–178).

6. Jeffrey Gray et al. (1983). Psychological and physiological relations between anxiety and impulsivity. In Marvin Zuckerman (ed.), *Biological bases of sensation seeking, impulsivity, and anxiety* (pp. 181–217). Hillsdale, NJ: Erlbaum.

7. Roger C. Schanck and Robert P. Abelson (1977). *Scripts, plans, and understanding* (p. 37). Hillsdale, NJ: Erlbaum.

8. L. V. Helms cited in Clifford Geertz (1983). *Local knowledge* (pp. 37–39). New York: Basic Books.

9. Cf. Sandra J. Hartman et al. (1988). The impact of occupation, performance, and sex on sex role stereotyping. *Journal of Social Psychology, 128*, 451–463.

10. Cf. David C. Funder and Daniel J. Ozer (1983). Behavior as a function of situation. *Journal of Personality and Social Psychology, 44*, 107–112.

11. Hans-George Voss and Heide Keller (1983). *Curiosity and exploration* (pp. 151, 156, 159). New York: Academic Press.

12. Albert A. Harrison and Mary M. Converse (1984). Groups in exotic environments. *Advances in Experimental Social Psychology, 18*, 49–87.

13. Cf. D. E. Berlyne (1960). *Conflict, arousal, and curiosity* (pp. 61–66). New York: McGraw-Hill.

14. Else Frenkel-Brunswick (1949). Intolerance of ambiguity as an emotional and perceptual personality variable. *Journal of Personality, 18*, 108–143.

15. R. H. Strotz (1956). Myopia and inconsistency in dynamic utility maximization. *Review of Economic Studies, 23*, 165–180.

16. David Bem (1981). Assessing situations by assessing persons. In Magnusson (ed.), op. cit. (pp. 245–257).

17. Brian T. Yates and Walter Mischel (1979). Young children's

192 NOTES

preferred attentional strategies for delaying gratification. *Journal of Personality and Social Psychology, 37,* 286–300.

18. Cf. Joseph Nuttin (1980). *Motivation et perspectives d'avenir* (chap. 1). Louvain: Presses Universitaires.

19. Cf. Mary K. Stevenson (1986). A discounting model for decisions with delayed positive or negative outcomes. *Journal of Experimental Psychology: General, 115,* 131–154.

20. Levon Melikian (1959). Preference for delayed reinforcement. *Journal of Social Psychology, 50,* 81–86.

21. Michael J. White (1985). Determinants of community satisfaction in Middletown. *American Journal of Community Psychology, 13,* 583–597.

22. J. W. Bardo and J. B. Hughey (1984). The structure of community satisfaction in a British and an American Community. *Journal of Social Psychology, 124,* 151–157.

23. Elsa M. Siipola (1935). A group study of some effects of preparatory set. *Psychological Monograph, 46,* n. 210, 27–38.

24. Peter J. McDonald and Scott A. Wooten (1988). The influence of incompatible responses on the reduction of aggression. *Journal of Social Psychology, 128,* 401–406.

25. Lionel Tiger (1979). *Optimism* (p. 15). New York: Simon & Schuster.

26. Julie K. Noren and Nancy Carter (1986). Anticipatory and post hoc cushioning strategies. *Cognitive Therapy and Research, 10,* 347–362.

27. Stephen Strack et al. (1987). Predicting successful completion of an aftercare program following the treatment for alcoholism. *Journal of Personality and Social Psychology, 53,* 579–584.

28. Michael F. Scheier et al. (1986). Coping with stress. *Journal of Personality and Social Psychology, 51,* 1257–1264. Charles S. Carver and Joan G. Gaines (1987). Optimism, pessimism, and postpartum depression. *Cognitive Therapy and Research, 11,* 449–462.

29. Sidney Pollard (1968). *The idea of progress* (pp. 182–184). London: Watts.

30. John Bartlett (1968). *Familiar quotations* (p. 983a). Boston: Little, Brown & Co.

31. Herbert C. Kelman and V. Lee Hamilton (1989). *Crimes of obedience.* New Haven: Yale University Press.

32. Alexander L. George (1980). *Presidential decision making in foreign policy* (pp. 152–153). Boulder, Col.: Westview Press. Abraham P. Lowenthal (1972). *The Dominican Intervention* (p. 161). Cambridge, MA: Harvard University Press.

33. Richard Nisbett and Lee Ross (1980). *Human inference* (p. 282). Englewood Cliffs, NJ: Prentice-Hall.

34. Ernest R. May (1973). *"Lessons" of the past* (pp. 52, 112–113). New York: Oxford University Press.

35. Peter Suedfeld and A. Dennis Rank (1976). Revolution leaders. *Journal of Personal and Social Psychology, 34,* 169–178.

36. Hendrick Smith (1988). The fight against Reagan. *New York Times,* 17 January 1988, VI, 36–39, 72, 77.

37. Cf. Robert Jervis (1970). *The logic of images in international relations* (e.g., pp. 5, 6, 20, 26, 30). Princeton: Princeton University Press.

38. Cf. Donald R. Kinger and David O. Sears (1985). Public opinion and political action. In Gardner Lindzey and Elliot Aronson (eds.), *Handbook of social psychology, 2,* (659–741). New York: Random House.

39. Joel Best and Gerald T. Horiuchi (1985). The razor blade in the apple. *Social Problems, 32,* 488–499.

40. Ted Gurr (1970). *Why men rebel* (pp. 281, 319). Princeton: Princeton University Press.

Chapter 7. Desirability and Value

1. American Psychiatric Association (1980). Diagnostic and statistical manual of mental disorders (pp. 292–298). Washington, DC: APA. Cf. Ernest S. Barratt (1972). Anxiety and impulsiveness. In Charles D. Spielberger (ed.), *Anxiety, 1,* (pp. 195–222). New York: Academic Press. Barratt (1983). Impulsivity. In Marvin Zuckerman (ed.), *Biological bases of sensation seeking, impulsivity, and anxiety* (pp. 77–116). Hillsdale, NJ: Erlbaum.

2. Michael Frese et al. (1987). Goal orientation and planfulness. *Journal of Personality and Social Psychology, 52,* 1122–1194.

3. S. B. G. Eysenck and H. J. Eysenck (1977). The place of impulsiveness in a dimensional system of personality. *British Journal of Social and Clinical Psychology, 16,* 57–68.

4. Arnold H. Buss and Robert Plomin (1975). *A temperamental theory of personality development* (p. 196). New York: Wiley.

5. Thomas Schill et al. (1985). Relation of expression of hostility to coping with stress. *Psychological Reports, 56,* 193–194.

6. Cf. George Ainslie (1975). Specious reward. *Psychological Bulletin, 82,* 463–496.

7. Aron W. Siegman (1961). The relationship between time perspective, time estimation, and impulse control in a group of young

offenders and in a control group. *Journal of Consulting Psychology*, *25*, 470–475.

8. Michael Schleifer and Virginia L. Douglas (1973). Moral Judgments, behaviour, and cognitive style in young children. *Canadian Journal of Behavioral Science, 5*, 133–144.

9. Samuel Croxall (1722). *Fables of Aesop, and others* (p. 63). Derby: Henry Mozley.

10. W. I. Thomas cited in Robert K. Merton (1957). *Social theory and social structure* (p. 475). New York: Free Press.

11. Allen F. Harrison and Robert M. Bramson (1982). *Styles of thinking* (p. 8). Garden City, NY: Anchor Press.

12. B. F. Skinner (1971). *Beyond freedom and dignity* (p. 26). New York: Knopf.

13. Robert Browning. *Andrea del Sarto.*

14. Kurt Lewin (1948). *Resolving social conflicts* (pp. 112–116). New York: Harpers.

15. *Idem.*, p. 103.

16. Michael F. Scheier et al. (1986). Coping with stress. *Journal of Personality and Social Psychology, 51*, 1257–1264.

17. Cited by John Gross (1987). Books of the Times. *New York Times*, Nov. 27, C31.

18. Eric Klinger (1971). *Structure and functions of fantasy* (pp. 6–10, 47, 49, 355). New York: Wiley-Interscience.

19. Cf. Harry Fowler (1965). *Curiosity and exploratory behavior* (pp. 31–33). New York: Macmillan.

20. Dean K. Simonton (1984). *Genius, creativity, and leadership.* (pp. 65–66, 181, 184, passim). Cambridge, MA: Harvard University Press.

21. Cf. Howard S. Becker (1960). Notes on the concept of commitment. *American Journal of Sociology, 66*, 32–40.

22. American Psychiatric Association, op. cit. (p. 220).

23. Cf. Fredrick Redlich and Daniel X. Freedman (1986). *The theory and practice of psychiatry* (pp. 2–3, 129, 252–253, 384, 509, 510). New York: Basic Books.

24. David Shakow (1963). Psychological deficit in schizophrenia. *Behavioral Science, 8*, 275–305.

25. Irwin P. Levin et al. (1988). The interaction of experiential and situational factors and gender in a simulated risky decision making task. *Journal of Psychology, 122*, 173–181.

26. Mark D. Rapport et al. (1986). Hyperactivity and frustration. *Journal of Abnormal Child Psychology, 14*, 191–204. Cf. Andrew Mil-

lar and Douglas J. Navarick (1984). Self-control and choice in humans. *Learning and motivation, 15*, 203–218.

27. Edwin A. Locke et al. (1968). Motivational effects of knowledge of results. *Psychological Bulletin, 70*, 474–485.

28. Robert J. Brandt and Donald M. Johnson (1955). Time orientation in delinquents. *Journal of Abnormal and Social Psychology, 51*, 343–345.

29. Cf. Lionel Tiger (1979). *Optimism* (pp. 20–21, 179). New York: Simon & Schuster.

30. Gregory Bateson (1972). *Steps to an ecology of mind* (pp. 494–505). New York: Ballantine Books.

31. Cf. Christopher Leone and Kevin Robertson (1989). Some effects of sex-linked clothing and gender schema on the stereotyping of infants. *Journal of Social Psychology, 129*, 609–619.

32. Connecticut Public Radio (1988). *All things considered* (September 30, 1988).

33. Peter S. Hawkins (1985). *Getting nowhere* (pp. 15–27). Cambridge, MA: Cowley.

34. Miquel de Unamuno (1926). *The tragic sense of life in men and in peoples* (pp. 139, 186, 193). London: Macmillan.

35. James J. Putnam (1917). *Human motives* (p. 65). Boston: Little, Brown & Co.

36. Ernest G. Schachtel (1959). *Metamorphosis* (p. 242). New York: Basic Books.

37. Daniel Kahneman and Amos Tversky (1972). Subjective probability. *Cognitive Psychology, 3*, 430–454.

38. Albert Bandura and Daniel Cervone (1983). Self-evaluative and self-efficacy mechanisms governing the motivational effects of goal systems. *Journal of Personality and Social Psychology, 45*, 1017–1028.

39. Cf. Allan Fenigstein et al. (1975). Public and private self-consciousness. *Journal of Consulting and Clinical Psychology, 43*, 522–527.

40. Cf. E. Lakin Philips (1951). Attitudes toward self and others. *Journal of Consulting Psychology, 15*, 79–81.

41. Zick, Rubin and Letitia A. Peplau (1975). Who believes in a just world? *Journal of Social Issues, 31*, n. 3, 65–89.

42. Philip J. Rossi (1983). *Together toward hope* (pp. 69, 75, 115, 158). Notre Dame: University of Notre Dame Press.

43. James W. Fowler (1981). *Stages of faith* (pp. xii, 133, 200, 290). New York: Macmillan.

44. Robert M. Tipton (1988). The effects of beliefs about smoking

and health on smoking cessation. *Journal of Psychology, 122,* 313–321.

45. Francisco Moreno (1977). *Between faith and reason* (especially pp. 74, 85, 94). New York: New York University Press.

46. Cf. Glynis M. Breakwell et al. (1988). The relationship of self-esteem and attributional style to young peoples' worries. *Journal of Psychology, 122,* 207–215.

47. Cf. Patricia Carpenter and Dennis P. Sugrue (1984). Psychoeducation in an outpatient setting. *Adolescence, 19,* 113–122.

Chapter 8. Training

1. Ulric Neisser (1967). *Cognitive psychology* (chaps. 3, 8). Englewood Cliffs, NJ: Prentice-Hall.

2. George A. Miller et al. (1960). *Plans and the structure of behavior* (p. 187). New York: Holt.

3. Cf. David C. Funder and Monica J. Harris (1986). Experimental effects and person effects in delay of gratification. *American Psychologist, 41,* 476–477.

4. Anthony Davids (1969). Ego functions in disturbed and normal children. *Journal of Consulting and Clinical Psychology, 33,* 61–70.

5. Cf. J. Holzi (1983). Der Einfluss der Impulsivität auf das Lösen von Analogieaufgaben. *Zeitschrift für Psychologie, 191,* 271–281.

6. I Samuel 17:39–51.

7. Alfred Jacobs and Milton Wolpin (1971). A second look at systematic desensitization. In Alfred Jacobs and Lewis B. Sachs (eds.), *The psychology of private events* (pp. 77–108). New York: Academic Press.

8. Stanley B. Messer (1976). Reaction and impulsivity. *Psychological Bulletin, 83,* 1026–1053.

9. Jerome Kagan et al. (1966). Modifiability of an impulsive tempo. *Journal of Educational Psychology, 57,* 359–365.

10. Susan W. Barstis and Leroy H. Ford (1977). Reaction-impulsivity, conservation, and the development of ability to control cognitive tempo. *Child Development, 48,* 953–959. Cf. Beth E. Kurtz and John G. Borkowski (1987). Development of strategic skills in impulsive and reflective children. *Journal of Child Psychology, 43,* 129–148.

11. Daniel Graybill et al. (1984). Remediation of impulsivity in learning disabled children by special education resource teachers using verbal self-instruction. *Psychology in the Schools, 21,* 252–254.

12. Regina M. Yondo and Jerome Kagan (1968). The effect of teacher tempo on the child. *Child Development, 39,* 27–34.

13. Stephen R. Briggs et al. (1980). An analysis of the self-monitoring scale. *Journal of Personality and Social Psychology, 38,* 679–86.

14. Graham B. Blaine (1962). *Patience and fortitude* (p. 200). Boston: Little, Brown & Co.

15. Walter G. Stephan (1985). Intergroup relations. In Gardner Lindzey and Elliot Aronson (eds.), *Handbook of social psychology* (pp. 599–658). New York: Random House.

16. Cf. John W. Atkinson (1958). Towards experimental analysis of human motivation in terms of motives, expectancies, and incentives. In John W. Atkinson (ed.), *Motives in fantasy, action, and society* (pp. 288–305). Princeton, NJ: Van Nostrand.

17. Cf. A. A. Bodalev (1975). On the study of some cognitive processes in Soviet social psychology. In Lloyd H. Strickland (ed.), *Soviet and western perspectives in Soviet psychology* (pp. 143–150). Oxford: Pergamon.

18. Dariusz Dolinski et al. (1987). Unrealistic pessimism. *Journal of Social Psychology, 127,* 511–516.

19. David H. Fischer (1971). *Historians' fallacies* (chaps. 1–3). London: Routledge & Kegan Paul.

20. George Florovsky (1969). The study of the past. In Ronald H. Nash (ed.), *Ideas of history* (pp. 351–369). New York: Dutton.

21. Patricia N. Limerick (1987). *The legacy of conquest* (p. 152). New York: Norton.

22. Cf. Israel Goldiamond (1965). Self-control procedures in behavior problems. *Psychological Reports, 17,* 851–868.

23. Walter B. Cannon (1976). The role of hunches. In Albert Rothenberg and Carl R. Hausman (eds.), *The creativity question* (pp. 63–69). Durham, NC: Duke University Press.

24. Geveviève Bramaud du Boucheron (1980). Compréhension de phrases décrivant des enévéments non familièrs chez des enfants de 4 à ans. *Bulletin de Psychologie, 35,* 635–642.

25. Johanna Shapiro and Deane H. Shapiro (1985). A "control" model of psychological health. *Sex Roles, 12,* 433–447.

26. Cf. Carl R. Rogers (1976). Toward a theory of creativity. In Rothenberg and Hausman, op. cit. (pp. 296–305).

27. Robert K. Merton (1957). *Social theory and social structure* (pp. 192–193, 476). New York: Free Press.

28. Cf. Lee Jussin (1986). Self-fulfilling prophecies. *Psychological Review, 93,* 429–445.

29. John Bartlett (1955). *Familiar quotations* (pp. 255, 341, 765). Boston: Little, Brown & Co.

30. Jeremy Bentham (1824). *The book of fallacies* (pp. 25, 32, 69, 127, 128, 156, 190, 198, 213, 258, 360). London: John and H. L. Hunt.

31. Leonard W. Doob (1948). *Public opinion and propaganda* (pp. 285–289). New York: Holt.

32. Richard Nisbett and Lee Ross (1980). *Human inference* (pp. 282–284). Englewood Cliffs, NJ: Prentice-Hall.

33. Irving L. Janis (1982). *Groupthink* (pp. 9–10, 14–47, 260–71). Boston: Houghton Mifflin.

34. Dennis L. Jennings et al. (1982). Informal covariation assessment. In Daniel Kahneman et al., *Judgment under uncertainty* (pp. 211–230). Cambridge, UK: Cambridge University Press.

35. Cf. Robyn M. Dawes (1982). The robust beauty of improper linear models in decision making. In Kahneman et al., op. cit. (pp. 391–407).

36. Cf. Baruch Fischoff (1982). Debiasing. In Kahneman et al., op. cit. (pp. 422–444).

37. Richard E. Nisbett et al. (1980). Improving inductive inference. In Kahneman, op. cit. (pp. 445–459).

38. Christopher R. Grace et al. (1988). Effects of compliance techniques on spontaneous and asked-for helping. *Journal of Social Psychology, 128*, 525–532.

39. Arthur L. Beaman (1988). Compliance as a function of elapsed time between first and second requests. *Journal of Social Psychology, 128*, 233–243.

40. Cf. Jean-Charles Chebat and Jacques Picard (1988). Receivers' self-acceptance and the effectiveness of two-sided messages. *Journal of Social Psychology, 128*, 353–362.

41. Cf. Timothy W. Smith et al. (1983). The self-serving function of hypochondriacal complaints. *Journal of Personality and Social Psychology, 44*, 787–797.

42. Cf. Scott J. Dickman (1988). Impulsivity and speed accuracy tradeoffs in information processing. *Journal of Personality and Social Psychology, 54*, 274–290.

43. Richard Katzev and Richard Brownstein (1989). The influence of enlightenment on compliance. *Journal of Social Psychology, 129*, 335–347.

44. Albert Bandura (1983). Self-efficacy determinants of anticipated fears and calamities. *Journal of Personality and Social Psychology, 45*, 464–469.

45. Cf. D. E. Berlyne (1960). *Conflict, arousal, and curiosity* (p. 187). New York: McGraw-Hill.

46. Howard Rachlin (1974). Self-control. *Behaviorism, 2,* 94–107.

47. Pamela Kenealy et al. (1988). Influence of children's physical attractiveness on teacher expectations. *Journal of Social Psychology, 128,* 373–383.

48. E. g., Stephen Toulmin (1961). *Foresight and understanding* (pp. 26–28, 99). Bloomington: Indiana University Press.

49. Fischer, op. cit. (p. 31).

50. Molly K. Reid and John G. Borkowski (1987). Causal attributions of hyperactive children. *Journal of Educational Psychology, 79,* 296–307.

51. Donald H. Meichenbaum and Joseph Goodman (1971). Training impulsive children to talk to themselves. *Journal of Abnormal Psychology, 77,* 115–126.

52. Tamar Zelniker (1973). Modification of information processing of impulsive children. *Child Development, 44,* 445–450.

53. David Shapiro (1965). *Neurotic styles* (pp. 134–140, 186–189). New York: Basic Books.

54. Lyle Tucker et al. (1987). Long-term hospital treatment of borderline patients. *American Journal of Psychiatry, 144,* 1443–1448.

55. Patricia Carpenter and Dennis P. Sugrue (1984). Psychoeducation in an outpatient setting. *Adolescence, 19,* 113–122.

56. B. F. Skinner (1953). *Science and human behavior* (pp. 230–241). New York: Free Press.

57. George Ainslie (1975). Specious reward. *Psychological Bulletin, 82,* 463–496.

58. Nisbett and Ross (1980), op. cit. (p. 280).

59. Cf. Goldiamond, op. cit.

60. Cf. Judy Genshaft (1983). A comparison technique to increase children's resistance to temptation. *Personality & Individual Differences, 4,* 339–341.

Recommended Readings

Bateson, Gregory (1972). *Steps to an ecology of mind*. New York: Ballantine.

Bentham, Jeremy (1824). *The book of political fallacies*. London: John & H. L. Hunt.

Berlyne, D. E. (1960). *Conflict, arousal, and curiosity*. New York: McGraw-Hill.

Brooke-Rose, Christine (1965). *A grammar of metaphor*. London: Secker & Warburg.

Brown, Roger (1958). *Words and things*. New York: Free Press.

Buss, Arnold H. and Robert Plomin (1975). *A temperamental theory of personality development*. New York: Wiley.

Dauenhauer, Bernard P. (1980). *Silence*. Bloomington: Indiana University Press.

Doob, Leonard (1971). *Patterning of time*. New Haven: Yale University Press.

Eysenck, Hans J. and Michael W. Eysenck (1985). *Personality and individual differences*. New York: Plenum.

Fischer, David H. (1971). *Historians' fallacies*. London: Routledge & Kegan Paul.

Fowler, Harry (1965). *Curiosity and exploratory behavior*. New York: Macmillan.

Fowler, James W. (1981). *Stages of faith*. San Francisco: Harper & Row.

Gergen, Kenneth J. (1982). *Toward transformation in social knowledge*. New York: Springer-Verlag.

Hall, Edward W. (1966). *The hidden dimension*. Garden City: Doubleday.

Harrison, Allen F. & Robert M. Bramson (1982). *Styles of thinking*. New York: Anchor.

Janis, Irving L. (1982). *Groupthink*. Boston: Houghton Mifflin.

Kagan, Jerome (1971). *Understanding children*. New York: Harcourt Brace Jovanovich.

Kahneman, Daniel; Paul Slovic; and Amos Tversky (1982). *Judgment under uncertainty*. Cambridge, UK: Cambridge University Press.

Kelman, Herbert C. and V. Lee Hamilton (1989). *Crimes of obedience*. New Haven: Yale University Press.

Magnusson, David (1981). *Toward a psychology of situations*. Hillsdale, NJ: Erlbaum.

Merton, Robert K. (1957). *Social theory and social structure*. New York: Free Press.

Moreno, Francisco J. (1977). *Between faith and reason*. New York: New York University Press.

Murray, Henry A. et al. (1938). *Explorations in personality*. New York: Oxford University Press.

Nisbett Richard and Lee Ross (1980). *Human inference*. Englewood Cliffs, NJ: Prentice Hall.

Nuttin, Joseph (1980). *Motivation et perspectives d'avenir*. Louvain: Presses Universitaires.

Peplau, Letitia A. and Daniel Perlman (1982). *Loneliness*. New York: Wiley

Pollard, Sidney (1968). *The idea of progress*. London: Watts.

Pollio, Howard R. (1974). *The psychology of symbolic activity*. Reading, MA: Addison-Wesley.

Richardson, Alan (1984). *The experiential dimension of psychology*. St. Lucia, Australia: University of Queensland Press.

Rokeach, Milton (1960). *The open and closed mind*. New York: Basic Books.

Schanck, Roger C. & Robert P. Abelson (1977). *Scripts, plans, goals, and understanding*. Hillsdale, NJ: Erlbaum.

Scheibe, Karl E. (1970). *Mirrors, masks, lies, and secrets*. New York: Praeger.

Simonton, Dean Keith (1984). *Genius, creativity, and leadership*. Cambridge, MA: Harvard University Press.

Toulmin, Stephen (1961). *Foresight and understanding*. Bloomington: Indiana University Press.

Voss, Hans-Georg & Heidi Keller (1983). *Curiosity and exploration*. New York: Academic Press.

Welford, A. T. (1980). *Reaction times*. London: Academic Press.

Zuckerman, Marvin (1983). *Biological bases of sensation seeking, impulsivity, and anxiety*. Hillsdale, NJ: Erlbaum.

Index

The page numbers in *italics* indicate the text pages on which a reference note is made without mentioning the author's name.

214 INDEX

About the Author

LEONARD DOOB is Sterling Professor of Psychology Emeritus and Associate Director, Southern African Research Program, at Yale University. He is the author of many books including *Inevitability* (Greenwood Press, 1988) and a host of journal articles.